In Their Hours of Ocean Leisure

In Their Hours of Ocean Leisure:

SCRIMSHAW
IN THE COLD SPRING HARBOR
WHALING MUSEUM

~

Richard C. Malley

1993
Whaling Museum Society
Cold Spring Harbor, New York

(516) 692-9626

This monograph has been published through generous grants
from The Banbury Fund and the New York State Council on the Arts.

COVER: *Carved whale ivory pie crimper with open heart design.*
6" (15.2 cm.). Source: *Weston Howland, 83.525*

Photographs by Michael M. Fairchild

Cataloging in Publication Data

Whaling Museum Society (Cold Spring Harbor, N.Y.)
    In their hours of ocean leisure : scrimshaw
in the Cold Spring Harbor Whaling Museum / Richard
C. Malley – [1st ed.]. – Cold Spring Harbor,
       p. : ill. ; cm.
    Bibliography: p.
    Includes index.

    1. Scrimshaw – Catalogs.   I. Malley, Richard C.
(Richard Christopher), 1952–   .   II. Title.

NK6022.W83
ISBN-0-9636361-0-3

Printed in the United States of America

To Kyle

Throughout the Pacific, and also in Nantucket, and New Bedford, and Sag Harbor, you will come across lively sketches of whales and whaling-scenes, graven by the fishermen themselves on Sperm Whale-teeth, or ladies' busks wrought out of the Right Whale-bone, and other like skrimshander articles, as the whalemen call the numerous little ingenious contrivances they elaborately carve out of the rough material, in their hours of ocean leisure.

Herman Melville, *Moby-Dick*

Contents

Foreword

The scrimshaw collection at the Cold Spring Harbor Whaling Museum has been admired and treasured locally by three generations of Long Islanders. Beyond a regional appreciation little is known about this important and extensive group of artifacts. In order to share the collection with a broader audience, the museum applied to the New York State Council on the Arts for funding to research and document the hundreds of examples of scrimshaw in its collection. We were pleased when Richard C. Malley, who had previously explored the scrimshaw collection at Mystic Seaport Museum, brought his expertise and wealth of knowledge to the task of documenting the scrimshaw holdings of this museum. We were also fortunate to have Michael M. Fairchild, grandson of Mrs. Tappen Fairchild, one of the Whaling Museum's founding Trustees, in the role of photographer for this monograph.

This publication was first conceived in 1984 by former Museum Director, Robert D. Farwell. It gives me great pleasure, as the current Executive Director, to see the project through to completion. We are particularly grateful to the New York State Council on the Arts for supporting the research and writing of this work, and to The Banbury Fund for so generously funding the publication of the monograph.

For those who have not seen this collection first hand, it is my hope they will enjoy a visual journey through the pages of this book. The author's research has brought a new appreciation for the collection as a whole, as well as valuable insights relative to some of the more unusual examples. Most importantly, he recognizes the significant role Long Island has played in the history of the American whale fishery. I believe that *In Their Hours of Ocean Leisure* ably fulfills the objective of introducing a marvelous collection to a larger, more diverse audience.

ANN M. GILL

Executive Director

Acknowledgments

Many individuals and institutions contributed to the writing and publication of this book. A generous grant from the New York State Council on the Arts funded the systematic cataloging of the scrimshaw collection. A second award from the Council helped support the writing of this monograph. In addition, major funding for this publication was provided through the generosity of The Banbury Fund.

Colleagues in other institutions in this country and abroad shared freely of their time and knowledge. In particular I wish to thank Linda Bailey of the Cincinnati Historical Society, Paul Cyr of the New Bedford Free Public Library, Peggy Dickerson of the Shelter Island Historical Society, Alfred Kleine-Kreutzmann of the Public Library of Cincinnati, Joöst Schokkenbroek of the Rijksmuseum Nederlands Scheepvaart Museum (Amsterdam), Robert Lloyd Webb of the Maine Maritime Museum, and Dr. Janet West of the Scott Polar Research Institute (Cambridge, England).

The staff at Mystic Seaport Museum was of tremendous help in furthering this project. I am especially grateful to Paul J. O'Pecko, Douglas Stein, and Dorothy Thomas who once again allowed me to make the G. W. Blunt White Library my second home; and to Peggy Tate Smith, Mary Anne Stets, and Claire White-Peterson in the photographic division.

The library staff of the Connecticut Historical Society was of great assistance during the research phase of this work. In particular I wish to thank Judith E. Johnson, Dr. Alesandra M. Schmidt, Ruth Blair, Kevin Quinn, and John Quinn for their patience in the face of constant requests.

I am also indebted to Weston Howland, Jr., for generously sharing information about his father's collecting activities, and to Dr. Geoffrey L. Rossano for his constructive suggestions. Longtime friend and colleague Dr. Margaret Vose freely shared her insights into many of the iconographic sources of this art. Credit also goes to Robert D. Farwell, the museum's former Director, who first proposed this project nearly a decade ago.

Finally, special thanks are due to those individuals most closely involved with this study. The Whaling

Museum staff was tremendously supportive, particularly Ann M. Gill, Executive Director, and Ina Katz, Curator. The considerable photographic skills of Michael Fairchild contributed materially to the value of this work. Thanks, too, are due to Andrew W. German for his editorial guidance and to the design talents of Mimmi and Lynn Scull. Lastly, I wish to thank my wife, Kyle M. Conard, whose advice, love, and patience helped stay the course.

RICHARD C. MALLEY
West Simsbury, Connecticut

A 1974 graduate of Providence College, Richard C. Malley received his M. A. in American history from Fordham University. Following ten years on the curatorial staff at Mystic Seaport Museum, he served as Curator of The Mariners' Museum in Newport News, Virginia. Since 1990 he has been Registrar of The Connecticut Historical Society.

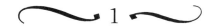

An Art Born of Adversity

First and Middle part these 24 hours calm. Latter part light breezes and pleasant weather. all hands employed scrimshonting. so ends this day. —no Whales and hard times.[1]

Among the earliest known recorded uses of the term "scrimshaw" is this passing reference, dated 14 March 1821, in an entry in the log of the whaling brig *Orion* of Rochester, Massachusetts. Commanded by Obed Luce, the 99-ton vessel had been cruising the whaling grounds near the Cape Verde Islands for nine months and its crew had only five sperm whales to show for their effort. The essence of this brief remark, variously repeated by keepers of logs and journals aboard hundreds of whaling vessels through much of the nineteenth century, goes to the heart of the folk art of scrimshaw. In response to extended periods of shipboard inactivity characteristic of the whale fishery, mariners turned to a variety of time-killing diversions, among them scrimshaw, to fill what Melville called "their hours of ocean leisure."

A Word About the Word

The ancestry of the term "scrimshaw" has been the source of long and lively debate, with various proponents claiming English, Dutch, Native American, Yankee, and even Norse origins.[2] Curiously, the concepts of carving, decoration, economy, or leisure implicit in these individual roots are, taken together, very close to what scrimshaw is generally recognized to be – *the activity of carving or engraving the ivory, bone and other by-products of certain marine mammals, and the use of these same materials in the fashioning of home-made items*. Of greater importance perhaps to readers of this study is the fact that the word applies equally to the multitude of *products* resulting from this activity.

Based on a review of the scrimshaw items in this and other collections, both public and private, some generalizations can be made about the practice and products of this art form. Scrimshaw is primarily a nineteenth-century phenomenon closely tied to the pelagic whale fishery. The vast majority of the work appears to be American in origin, not surprising considering the overwhelming size of the American whaling fleet in comparison with those of other nations. British,

European – and even Australian[3] – whalemen clearly practiced this art as well, though due to similarities of form and design much of their work has been assumed to be of American origin. In general, the amount of scrimshaw work appears to be in direct proportion to the size of the whale fishery at a given time; in terms of quantity the period 1820–60 – when as many as twenty thousand whalemen might have been employed annually in the American fleet alone – was probably the most productive.

Although scrimshaw is primarily associated with the whale fishery there are examples of work done on board merchant ships and other types of vessels. A corset busk in the Mystic Seaport Museum collection, for example, is engraved "On Board the Ship B.F. Hoxie." This medium clipper transshipped a cargo of whale oil and baleen from Honolulu to New York in 1856.[4] Even more unusual is the identity of the scrimshander – Mary Stark, the captain's wife. Though less commonly, scrimshaw has also been pursued aboard naval vessels.[5]

By and large, scrimshaw is an anonymous art; in most cases scrimshanders left their work unsigned.[6] But while only a very small percentage of examples bear signatures, in recent years much effort has been spent in stylistic comparison of pieces in both public and private collections. As a result it has been possible in some cases to make attributions based on careful comparison with signed examples.[7]

The Motivation

The anonymous nature of so much scrimshaw can be traced back to the conditions which prompted its practice. Edwin P. Brown, master of the bark *Noble* of New Suffolk, Long Island, lamented, "The Scene Now Before me pre-sents a very dark aspect. Four monts out today. Not one whale have we taken yet."[8] Even after the first whale was taken long dry spells frequently occurred. Such extended periods of forced inactivity prompted one bored New London whaleman to observe, "all hands Employed in doing nothing but growl at one another."[9] There was only so much painting, tarring, sail repair, and other forms of "ship's duty" to occupy the large crews while waiting for the next appearance of the elusive prey. Time weighed heavily, especially during the globe-girdling, multi-year voyages that became the rule in the American industry in the second quarter of the nineteenth century. The need to pass time encouraged the practice of various arts, from fancy ropework to the decorative carving of scraps of wood. The availability of raw materials like whale teeth, panbone, and baleen aboard whaling vessels ensured their use as well, resulting in the art form that has come to be termed scrimshaw.

Since, for many, scrimshaw was first and foremost a means of coping with adversity rather than a conscious effort to create a lasting work of art, it is not surprising that most examples went unsigned. Even in those instances when a whaleman created a piece as a gift for a loved one it is rare to find a signature.

Among the whaleman's basic shipboard skills was the use of knives, awls, needles, fids, and other tools. Familiarity with, and constant use of, tools meant that most seamen had the rudimentary dexterity required to undertake the sanding, carving, and engraving basic to the art of scrimshaw. For the first-time whalemen, referred to as "greenhands," advice and encouragement could be had from their more experienced shipmates. Some of the latter equipped themselves with what Melville termed "dentistical-looking implements," and

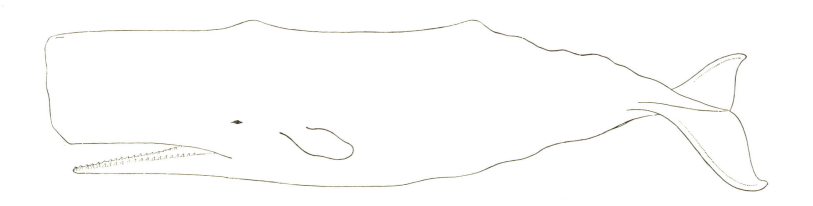

**1. The sperm whale's massive lower jaw provided both teeth and panbone
for the scrimshander. From The Fisheries and Fishery Industries of the United States, 1884.**
Photograph courtesy of Mystic Seaport Museum, Inc.

others, notably ships' officers or carpenters, sometimes had access to lathes for elaborate turning work. Occasionally evidence surfaces of a whaleman's first attempts at scrimshaw. The journal of Lucy Hix Crapo, the wife of the master of the bark *Louisa*, contains the following entry for 6 August 1866: "Received a present of a pair of engraved whale's teeth from F. Thomas, the cook – his first attempt at such work."[10] Gurdon Hall, a greenhand aboard the whaleship *Charles Phelps* of Stonington, Connecticut, noted in his journal that the ship's master (who was, incidentally, his uncle) "turned me one Cane head," and that he, in return, "Marked a Busk for him."[11] Many whalemen, however, relied on basic tools like saws, files, awls, sail needles, and knives in pursuing this off duty calling.

Raw Materials

Basic to our definition of scrimshaw is the use of certain marine mammal by-products, primarily generated by the activity of whaling. An appreciation of the scrimshander's achievements depends on a basic understanding of the source and nature of these unusual materials.

The sperm whale [1] is perhaps the species most familiar to readers, thanks in large part perhaps to *Moby-Dick*. It was also one of the most familiar to whalemen, an aggressive and elusive prey valued both for the high quality of oil rendered from its blubber and a waxy substance called spermaceti (used in candles) found in a cavity in its head. One of the few toothed whale species

2. Whaleman Robert Weir's 1855–58 journal kept aboard the bark Clara Bell
included this sketch showing the removal of teeth from the jaw of a sperm whale.
Courtesy of Mystic Seaport Museum, Inc.

actively hunted, its long, narrow lower jaw is equipped with up to four dozen hard, heavily ridged teeth. Corresponding sockets in the upper jaw allow the sperm whale to seize prey such as squid.

During the processing or "cutting in" of a sperm whale the head was removed from the body and hoisted on deck. At some point the teeth were pried from the gum and bone of the lower jaw [2] and distributed among the crew. Only rarely were these opaque, fine-grained teeth, called "whale ivory," deemed of any commercial value.[12]

The close-grained skeletal bone of the sperm whale's lower jaw also provided a marvelous raw material. Called "panbone" after the large jaw pans of the whale, this material was utilized in making such decorative items as plaques bearing whaling scenes or other images. Its versatility and durability led to widespread use in a host of functional items, including corset busks, boxes, winding swifts, canes, and tools.

Filter-feeding species like the right and bowhead whales [3] lack teeth. Instead, large overlapping plates of a fibrous material called baleen hang from the roof of the mouth, forming a sievelike device for capturing krill and other small prey. In addition to great quantities of oil, a single baleen whale could yield hundreds or even

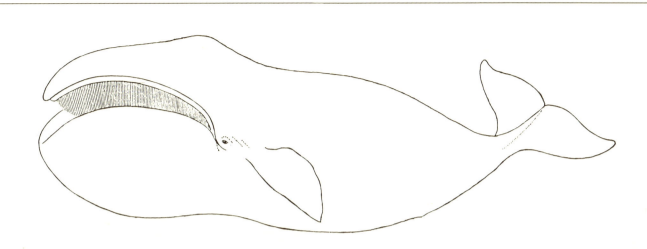

3. *Toothless species like the bowhead (top) and right whale used overlapping plates of baleen to filter food from the water. Although baleen is composed of keratin, like human fingernails, whalemen called it "whalebone." By whatever name, scrimshanders put this flexible material to good use. From* **The Fisheries and Fishery Industries of the United States, 1884.**
Photograph courtesy of Mystic Seaport Museum, Inc.

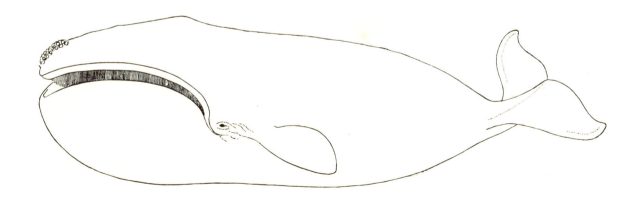

4. The Pacific walrus provided another source of raw material in the form of massive tusks. From The Fisheries and Fishery Industries of the United States, 1884.
Photograph courtesy of Mystic Seaport Museum, Inc.

thousands of pounds of this commercially valuable, lightweight substance, providing the scrimshander with another raw material. Although baleen (which the whale-men called "whalebone" or "bone") did not provide the easiest surface to engrave, this dark material was widely used for making boxes, busks, and other useful items.

Another raw material, walrus tusks, came into widespread use after the development of the Arctic whale fishery in the 1840s. Sometimes, if whales were scarce, whalemen would hunt the animals [4] among the ice floes and rocky islands of the northern Pacific. One whaling master's wife recorded in her journal, "The ships crew been down after walrus – succeeded in catching twenty."[13] At other times the long ivory tusks were acquired through trade, as one whaleman noted: "At 12 M. Made the isl of Nuvnivak. At 4 pm Natives came off to trade ivory."[14] With lengths of up to thirty inches or more, walrus tusks provided both a splendid medium for engraving and a source of large dimensional material for carved or turned objects such as pie crimpers and winding swifts.

Smaller whales like the pilot whale or "blackfish" also provided a source of raw material in the form of the lower jaw, which was sometimes engraved in the manner of a sperm whale's mandibles. Further, as an alternative to salt beef and other poor provisions whalemen would occasionally harpoon porpoises as the swift mammals paced the vessel. Besides providing a welcome change of fare (and sometimes a lightweight oil from the blubber) the lower jaw could also be engraved.

A wide range of other materials found their way into scrimshaw items. Wood species from common cedar and pine to more exotic tropical hardwoods were frequently employed, primarily in functional objects. Coconut shells, mother-of-pearl and abalone, horn, tortoiseshell, metal – even colored sealing wax – provided contrasting color and texture in combination with ivory, panbone, or baleen.

Basic Techniques

. . . got up A couple of Sperm Teeth. Scraped them off Smooth Ready to polish – have Some Idea of Scratching A Little Something on them to make them look as Curious As possible . . . [15]

In recording these lines aboard the whaleship *Charles Phelps*, Gurdon Hall highlighted several techniques basic to the art of scrimshaw. The heavily ridged whales teeth [5] needed to be smoothed and polished before any decorative work could commence. Using knives, files, saws, and abrasives a suitable surface and shape could be prepared. A pencil sketch of the proposed design might be made on the surface before an engraving tool such as a knife or needle created the incising. Many designs, especially those featuring women's portraits, were copied from published illustrations using a tracing method called "pin-pricking." By making tiny pin pricks with needle or stylus along the outline of an attached engraving or other illustration, and then connecting the dots, a faithful copy of the original design could be achieved. Once the scrimshander was satisfied with the design (and mistakes and corrections were common) a contrasting liquid or dry pigment was applied and quickly wiped off. The residue in the engraved areas made the image visible. The same technique was used with decorated walrus tusks and panbone slabs. Besides inks of various colors, potential pigments are believed to have included such forms of carbon as lampblack and charcoal, as well as copper oxide and various natural dyes from plants and berries.

5. The heavily-ridged surface of a raw sperm whale tooth (top) needed preparation before engraving could commence, 7⅛ in. (18.1 cm.); once smoothed (bottom) the scrimshander's work could begin in earnest, 8⅛ in. (20.7 cm.).
Source: Anonymous, 83.340, 83.203

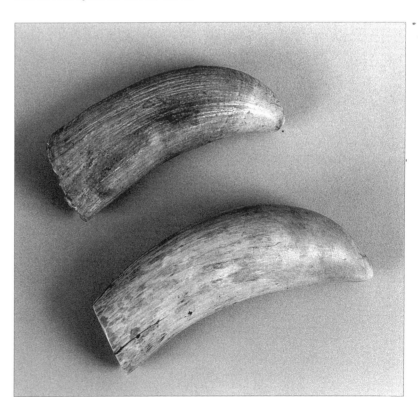

Panbone from the jaw of the sperm whale was variously sawed, filed, planed, turned, and steamed and bent in the creation of both decorative panbone plaques and a bewildering variety of functional items. In many cases panbone served the same purpose as wood, and was similarly handled.

The flexible properties that made baleen valuable in corsets, umbrellas, and other manufactured goods was also utilized by the scrimshander. Once cleaned, dried, and cut down to workable size this thin material, like panbone, could be heated and bent for use in ditty boxes, sliced into strips for corset busks, or cut into different shapes for use as inlay in canes, pie crimpers, boxes, swifts, and a multitude of other items. Boxes and busks in particular were also engraved with a wide variety of decorative motifs. Occasionally a light-colored pigment might be applied to enhance the contrast of the engraving against the dark surface.[16]

2

Between Sea and Sound

Paumanok [1]
Sea-beauty! stretch'd and basking!
One side thy inland ocean laving, broad, with copious
    commerce, steamers, sail,
And one the Atlantic's wind caressing, fierce or gentle —
    mighty hulls dark-gliding in the distance.
Isle of sweet brooks of drinking water — healthy air and soil!
Isle of the salty shore and breeze and brine!

Walt Whitman, *Leaves of Grass*

An Island People

Just as the folk art form known as scrimshaw flourished within the context of the whaling industry, so was whaling part of a larger mosaic of American maritime activity beginning in the seventeenth century. This was true of mainland towns like New Bedford and New London, and equally so of Long Island ports. Even a cursory survey of Long Island's maritime achievements shows that the island's nineteenth-century whaling activity was less a fundamental revolution than a logical evolution, built on a common heritage of regional ties and experiences.

An inescapable fact is that Long Island is an *island*. Until the development of bridge and tunnel links to the mainland in the late nineteenth and early twentieth cen-

turies, this reality helped determine its political, social, and economic course. The coastal and ocean waters that fixed the island's boundaries provided both a medium of transportation and communication and a source of livelihood for thousands of Long Islanders.

The proximity of Long Island to the New England colonies, especially Connecticut and Massachusetts, forged early ties that in some ways survive into modern times. Despite the Dutch presence at New Amsterdam much of eastern Long Island was, in fact, part of Connecticut, and many settlers relocated from across the Sound. The establishment of the colony of New York after the 1664 defeat of the Dutch may have changed the political boundaries, but not necessarily the traditional social and economic ties of many islanders. In fact, during the American Revolution thousands fled the British occupation of Long Island, crossing the Sound in small boats to exile in Connecticut, where so many families had their roots.

Strong ties with the mainland to the north prompted the development of a water-borne communication and transportation network that included sailing packets and, as early as 1739, scheduled ferry service.[2] The latter venture, crossing from Matinecock to a point near Rye, utilized a horse-powered craft. Though a 1741 storm claimed this pioneering vessel and its owner, Major Thomas Jones,[3] it marked the beginning of a system that, though peaking in the early 1900s, continues to this day.

Ubiquitous packet sloops provided both scheduled and unscheduled service between such Long Island villages as Sag Harbor, Huntington, and Oyster Bay and mainland ports like Newport, Providence, New London, New Haven, Middletown, Hartford, and New York. Beginning in 1815 the miracle of steam propulsion was adopted on the sheltered waters of the Sound and its tributaries, freeing passengers and cargoes from the vagaries of wind and tide and further strengthening links to southern New England.[4] However, communication with New York became more important as that city grew into the leading entrepôt in the young United States. Until the Long Island Railroad reached Greenport in 1844, the fastest means of travel to New York from eastern Long Island was by packet sloop, a journey of approximately two days.[5]

Even after the arrival of the railroad, water transportation remained the most economical means of shipping bulk goods like the hay, flour, cordwood, and bricks produced by Long Island's agrarian economy; and returning the manure, ashes, and lumber required on the farms and in the growing towns on the island.[6] Long Island's once flourishing coasting trade, with roots dating back to the 1600s, survived into the early twentieth century, until the few remaining schooners succumbed to the combination of steamers, railroads, and trucks.

The demands of an island people for transportation and communication spurred the development of shipbuilding from an early date. The need to export agricultural staples to the other American colonies, and particularly the Caribbean islands, and to import English manufactured goods, West Indian molasses, and other products, contributed to the rise of Long Island shipbuilding. Local maritime enterprise, devastated during the American Revolution, was rekindled by the postwar national economic recovery. Shipyards in such north shore settlements as Cold Spring Harbor, Northport, and, later, Port Jefferson, as well as Sag Harbor, rose to the challenge, overtaking colonial shipbuilding centers such as Oyster Bay.[7] New trades like those to the Caribbean and Central America for logwood, coffee, and fruit demanded more Long Island-built vessels,[8] notably brigs and schooners. The growth of the island's fin- and shellfisheries likewise contributed to the development of the shipbuilding industry as yards large and small responded to the increasing demand for craft to harvest the riches of the sea.

Both the open ocean and the sheltered waters of bay, creek, and Sound provided the basis for a thriving fishing industry. Seasonal pursuits like the menhaden harvest supplemented farm and other incomes into the twentieth century, when Long Island was still a leader in this specialized fishery.[9] Oystering too was a seasonal undertaking until the nineteenth century when it was organized, mechanized, and to some extent industrialized to meet increasing market demand.[10]

A Whaling Heritage

Long Island's first whaling activities were shore based and bore little resemblance to the later industry. The island's location on the migratory route of certain whales prompted Native Americans, especially the Shinnecock and Montauk tribes, to pursue the mammals along the shore. It is suggested by some that Basque whalers, who established temporary camps along the North American coast in the sixteenth century, first introduced whaling techniques to the tribes.[11] By whatever means it occurred, when the island's first European settlers arrived they found an established shore whaling tradition.

English settlers saw shore whaling as a valuable seasonal supplement to farming. Whaling companies were formed by town governments, initially in the Southampton area, and the first private company was organized in 1650. Skilled Native American whalemen served in many of these colonial boat crews, foreshadowing their descendants' participation in the pelagic whale fishery nearly two centuries later. The fledging industry clearly prospered: 2,148 barrels of whale oil were recorded by Southampton and East Hampton whaling companies in 1687, a total that nearly doubled within twenty years.[12]

Despite the fact that Long Island shore whaling continued until the early twentieth century, by the mid-1700s a marked decline was noted. Whether from depletion of whale stocks or natural variations in the migration and feeding habits of the right and humpback whales, the industry seemed to be dying. But a change was in the offing that would rescue – and fundamentally alter the nature of – American whaling.

Long Island and the American Whale Fishery

Although some evidence suggests Long Islanders organized an offshore whaling venture based on Roanoke Island, North Carolina, as early as 1667,[13] the systematic pursuit of deep-sea whales by Americans began in Massachusetts, especially on Cape Cod and, after 1715, the island of Nantucket. Long Island's first, tentative steps toward offshore whaling were not taken until 1760.

In the colonial era the small port of Sag Harbor developed primarily for shipping produce from eastern Long Island. In 1760 several local merchants, no doubt eyeing Nantucket's whaling successes, dispatched the sloops *Goodluck, Dolphin*, and *Success* to cruise for right whales off the North Carolina coast around latitude 36°N.[14] The success of this first venture is unknown, and though there is but scant evidence of further Sag Harbor whaling activity until 1784, it seems highly probable that other, unrecorded voyages were made in the ensuing years. It is possible that some records were lost during the Revolution, when whaleboat raids from Connecticut attacked the occupying British forces at Sag Harbor,[15] or in the devastating fires that struck the port in 1817 and 1845.

With peace came a revival of maritime activity on Long Island. While the coasting trade initially put Sag Harbor back on its feet, whaling made the village known in ports around the globe. The 1784 departure of the ship *Hope*, the first Long Island whaleship equipped with try-works to process whales at sea, marked the beginning of a new phase in the evolution of both the port and the island. Through the next forty-five years Sag Harbor

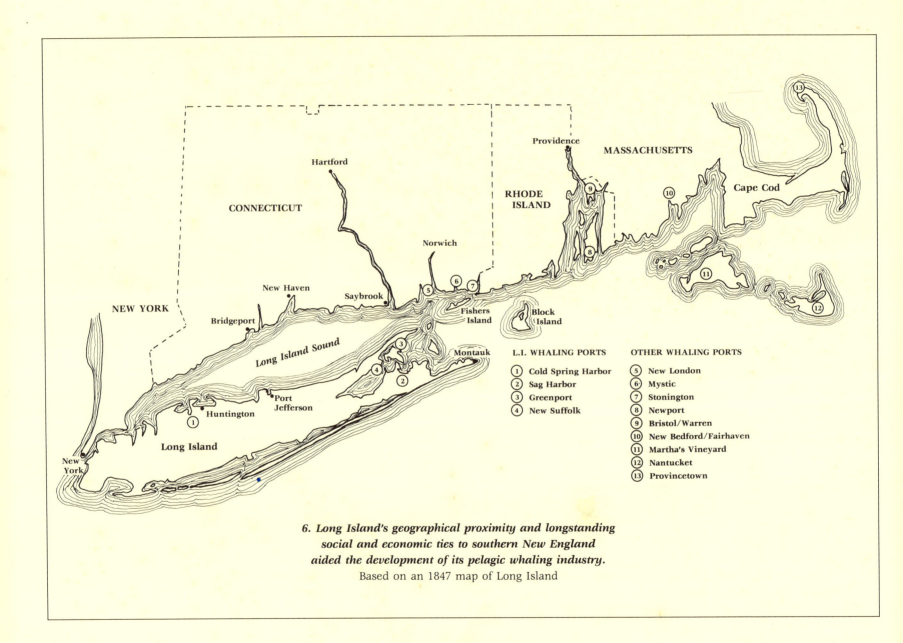

L.I. WHALING PORTS

① Cold Spring Harbor
② Sag Harbor
③ Greenport
④ New Suffolk

OTHER WHALING PORTS

⑤ New London
⑥ Mystic
⑦ Stonington
⑧ Newport
⑨ Bristol/Warren
⑩ New Bedford/Fairhaven
⑪ Martha's Vineyard
⑫ Nantucket
⑬ Provincetown

6. Long Island's geographical proximity and longstanding
social and economic ties to southern New England
aided the development of its pelagic whaling industry.

Based on an 1847 map of Long Island

remained Long Island's sole whaling port, steadily building up its fleet of ships and barks.

The boom decades of the 1830s and 1840s prompted other Long Island towns to enter the whaling business [6]. Greenport's first whaler sailed in 1830, commencing three decades of activity for that village. Cold Spring Harbor was not far behind. Its first vessel, the bark *Monmouth*, sailed in 1836, albeit from Sag Harbor.[16] At least nine whaling voyages were made from tiny New Suffolk during the period 1838–50, and possibly several from nearby Jamesport.[17] At the peak of the industry in the mid-1840s Sag Harbor alone counted some fifty whalers in its fleet at one time, while Greenport boasted no fewer than a dozen. Cold Spring Harbor's fleet peaked in 1845, when eight ships and barks were engaged in the trade.

Long Island whalemen had early specialized in the northern and southern Atlantic right whale fisheries, in contrast to New Bedford and Nantucket's emphasis on the sperm whale. In time the vast Pacific grounds attracted Long Island whaleships as well. The search for new concentrations of whales led to the discovery of the Northwest Coast grounds, off British Columbia and Washington Territory. Among the first whaleships to declare for this new area was the ship *Daniel Webster* of Sag Harbor, sailing in 1841.[18] Within a few years the explosive growth of the American whaling fleet was depleting whale stocks in most of the known grounds, including the Northwest Coast. Thus when Captain Thomas Welcome Roys sailed the Sag Harbor bark *Superior* through the Bering Straits in 1848, discovering vast numbers of bowhead whales, it proved a salvation to the industry.[19]

Long Island's whaling industry, though dwarfed by New Bedford's, surpassed that of many other important whaling ports. The business supported ship- and boat-

7. *Sag Harbor was the undisputed leader among Long Island whaling ports. Engraving from Barber's* **Historical Collections of the State of New York, 1841.**
Courtesy of The Connecticut Historical Society

builders, coopers, sailmakers, ship chandlers, and a host of other craftsmen and merchants ashore. Perhaps more importantly, whaling helped broaden the island's predominantly agricultural economic base. While this was especially true of Sag Harbor [7], from which nearly six hundred voyages were made, secondary ports like Greenport and Cold Spring Harbor, together accounting for more than 130 sailings, also contributed to the ongoing transformation of Long Island.[20]

Capital from whaling found its way into various manufacturing and transportation concerns. In fact, the precipitous decline of Long Island's whaling industry in the 1850s was due as much to a flow of capital and labor to newer, more lucrative ventures as it was to the disruption caused by the 1849 gold rush or declining numbers of whales. The development of petroleum and the disruption of the Civil War came too late to exert any real effect on the moribund Long Island whaling industry.[21] The fishery was hardly more than a memory by the time Long Island's last whaling vessel sailed in 1871.

The impact of whaling on Long Island was more than economic. The fraternity of whalemen knew no bounds of race or nationality, and Long Island boys learned their trade serving alongside men from other states and nations. Many sailed on Long Island vessels while others signed aboard whalers from a dozen different ports, as close as New London and as distant as Honolulu. African-Americans, together with descendants of earlier Native American shore whalemen, joined eager farm boys in the common experience of life before the mast and, more importantly, in the whaleboat where teamwork and trust went hand in hand.[22] By requiring such dependence among its mixed crews, whaling generated a grudging respect for ability over race or economic position not always seen back home.

Long Island Whaling as History

As industrialization in the east and expansion in the west held the nation's attention into the new century, appreciation of the past maritime achievements of the nation faded. However, a revival of interest in maritime history developed in the twenties and thirties. Though artists and writers contributed to this phenomenon nationally, it was on the local level that some of the most important steps were taken. Along the coast, primarily in the northeast, a series of local museums was born, each dedicated to preserving the maritime history of their respective areas. The end of the American whale fishery in the 1920s sparked a special interest in this branch of maritime enterprise. For Long Island, 1936 was a banner year, as two public collections were begun, one at Sag Harbor, and the other, the focus of this study, in Cold Spring Harbor.

A Collection is Born

While the Whaling Museum Society of Cold Spring Harbor dates its founding to 1936, it owes its existence to a 1912–13 whaling voyage aboard the Long Island-built brig *Daisy*. Dr. Robert Cushman Murphy (1887–1973) [8], a young naturalist who later gained worldwide fame as an authority on oceanic birds, spent the better part of a year aboard the *Daisy* observing and participating in the hunt for sperm whales. A whaleboat from the vessel, acquired by Murphy in the hope of installing it in a whaling exhibit, was eventually offered to Cold Spring Harbor in 1942.[23] The rest, as they say, is history.

Like a magnet, the fledgling museum attracted objects and manuscripts that chronicled centuries of Long Island maritime history. From local parlors and attics flowed a stream of material documenting Long Island whaling, coastal commerce, shipbuilding, and related pursuits.

The scrimshaw collection, now numbering hundreds of items, forms an integral part of the museum's holdings. But the scrimshaw differs from the rest of the collection in that it, like the industry that spawned it, represents the work of whalemen and sailors from different regions, most of whom remain anonymous. It is especially appropriate, though, that one of the handful of identified scrimshanders represented in the collection is Robert Cushman Murphy.

The basis of the museum's scrimshaw collection was a series of gifts from Long Island donors, beginning shortly after the completion of the museum building in 1942. Several whale teeth and a baleen busk were included in the first acquisitions. Among the earliest donors was Miss Mary J. Holmes, a niece of whalemen Samuel and West Mitchell. She learned of scrimshaw firsthand through her uncles and their colleagues, acquiring pieces that would one day help form the nucleus of the collection. Other donors included scientists Captain Marion Eppley, U.S.N., and Robert Cushman Murphy.

The pattern of small gifts or purchases of scrimshaw was interrupted in 1956 when Weston Howland, a Massachusetts textile executive, offered a group of nearly three hundred pieces to the museum. A New Bedford native and descendant of whalemen, Howland recognized the importance of this art form and in the 1930s began actively acquiring both single pieces and entire family collections in the New Bedford area.[24] Through his generosity the museum's collection grew to become one of the largest public holdings in the state, boasting examples of many of the basic decorative and functional expressions of this art form.

The rapid growth of the scrimshaw collection seen in the 1940s and 1950s slowed considerably in the following decades. Many older private collections had either already been donated to museums or were sold, and a new, active generation of collectors took to the field. As market prices for scrimshaw increased, donations to museums fell off markedly. Since then only occasional gifts, like a superb pair of walrus tusks in the recently acquired Hewlett Collection that are attributed to local whaleman Manuel Enos, have been added to the Cold Spring Harbor collection.

8. Robert Cushman Murphy (1887–1973) provided the spark that helped create the Cold Spring Harbor Whaling Museum.
Cold Spring Harbor Whaling Museum collection

Clearly the days of passive collecting are over. The refinement of the museum's collection will require both a new, more critical view of the current holdings and a more active approach to new acquisitions. The 1990 purchase of a splendid engraved strip of baleen that is almost certainly the work of a Long Island whaleman exemplifies this new collecting course, one firmly grounded in solid research. This, combined with the recent wave of scholarship in the field of scrimshaw studies, will assist the museum in its continuing commitment to interpreting the life of the whaleman.

3

"Lively Sketches"
The Whaleman as Artist

I polished a pair of teeth for marking. So ends this day.[1]

This cryptic comment in the journal of whaleman Wilson Andrews of the New Bedford ship *Hibernia* leaves us hungering for more information. What *kind* of "marking" did Andrews execute on this pair of sperm whale teeth? Were they whaling scenes, vessel portraits, or perhaps depictions of the fairer sex? The answer remains a mystery, as he never mentioned the teeth again.

A wide array of engraved or carved images can be found on sperm whale teeth, walrus tusks, panbone and baleen panels, and other purely decorative examples of scrimshaw. Some reflect the scrimshander's intimate knowledge of seafaring and whaling and, by extension, his pride in it. Other subjects suggest a yearning for faraway things such as home, family, or the company of women. Still other designs express concepts like patriotism, religious faith, or love of nature.

Of Whaling and Seafaring

An iconographic survey of the collection shows many of the major thematic categories represented. Among them is that of whales; which seems only fitting as these creatures provided not only much of a scrimshander's raw materials, but more importantly his livelihood. But even in the best of times whales could be elusive. Henry Rogers, sailing aboard the ship *New England* in 1858, understood this when he observed that he and his crewmates were "Employed in waiting for whales to show themselves."[2] Even spotting whales was no guarantee of success. The logkeeper aboard the Cold Spring Harbor bark *Alice* noted with no little chagrin:

> We saw a Grait number of Ships to Day and We Saw one Whail and he Was a Going So fast that i think he Was Carrying the Mail i should like he Wood Stop and let us now where he is a Going.[3]

While whales obviously appear in whaling scenes, several teeth in the collection make sperm whales the sole subject. The most unusual of these is a small sperm whale tooth [9] engraved on one side with four grinning whales dancing in line. The caption "WHEN ZEB PLAYS HIS BANJO" seemingly explains the festivities. Although at

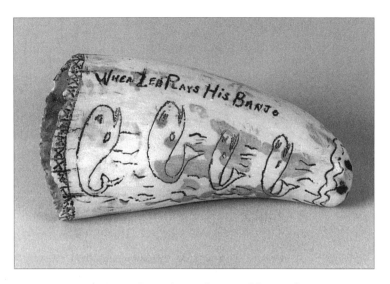

9. Whimsy or fact? The "Zeb" tooth poses this question, 4 in. (10.2 cm.).
Source: Weston Howland, 83.307

quality of the work may vary, the central message common to all of these pieces is that this was extraordinary work pursued by ordinary men. Whaling scenes abound on scrimshaw examples in the Cold Spring Harbor collection. Among these are a splendid matched pair of teeth [*10*], almost certainly the work of a British whaleman. The first of these, engraved "Whaling" in flowing script, shows two whaleboats from a British whaleship in quest of a sperm whale. Its mate, similarly engraved "Cutting In," illustrates the successful conclusion of the hunt. A combination of leaf-and-tendril and repeat geometric patterns create borders for each scene. Deep incising of the whaleship's port-painted hull contributes an added dimension to the whaling vignettes.

first glance one is inclined to pooh-pooh this tooth as nothing more than whimsy, research has shown that shipboard music can attract whales under certain conditions.[4] Further, by the mid-1800s the banjo was a common instrument in the fo'c'sle of many a vessel.[5] Perhaps the banjo-picking whaleman Zeb had some success in this line.

Since scrimshaw depended almost entirely on the activity of whaling, both for a motivation and a supply of raw materials, the whaling scene naturally became one of the dominant themes of the whaleman-artist. Just as the occasional whaleman's journal contains sketches of whaling activity, so also do many examples of this specialized art form. The dangers and the glory of what was perhaps the most demanding maritime pursuit of the age are chronicled on tooth, tusk, bone, and baleen. While the

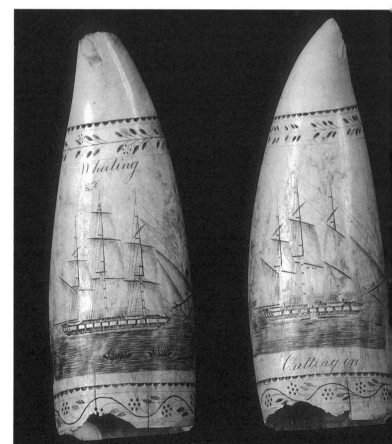

Thin slabs of panbone, cut from a sperm whale's jaw, provided a larger canvas for another whaleman. In one example [11] the last thirty inches of a whale's jaw was cut off and its smoothed surface engraved with a scene featuring a full-rigged whaleship. One of the three whaleboats in the hunt has been wrecked or "stove" as the hunted momentarily became the hunter. Such occurances were common when a wounded sperm whale attacked its tormentors. In such instances the huge jaws and impressive teeth so favored by the scrimshander could be turned upon him with deadly effect.

Once a whale was killed it was towed back to the vessel and secured, normally on the starboard side. The butchering or, in whaleman's parlance, "cutting-in" then began, with the officers using sharp, long-handled spades. Stripping the thick blubber from a whale resembled peeling an apple; large strips called "blanket pieces" were hoisted on deck using large hooks rigged to block and

10. *This matched pair of teeth illustrating two phases of whaling is probably the work of a British whaleman, 5⅞ in. (15 cm.).*
Source: Rodney Williams, 83.335.1–2

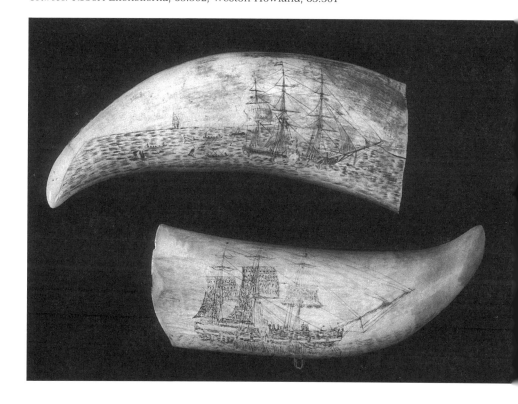

13. *Two examples of scrimshaw ship portraiture.* **Above, a British merchant vessel in its "frame," 6¼ in. (15.9 cm.). Below, what might be a Hawaiian whaleship,** **7¼ in. (18.5 cm.).**
Sources: Anonymous, 83.365; Robert Ekenstierna, 83.362

tackle. The blubber was then sliced into progressively smaller pieces until being placed in the iron trypots for rendering into oil. Two teeth in the collection [12] vividly illustrate this gruesome, bloody, greasy, and exhausting procedure. While both examples show the blanket piece being hoisted onto deck, one also includes an active whale hunt astern of the ship, perhaps as a reminder of the more glorious aspects of the fishery.

It is clear that the whaleman in the fo'c'sle looked at teeth, bone, and other whaling by-products much as the marine artist in his studio looked at canvas. These leftovers of the whale fishery afforded the scrimshander a wonderful surface for depicting vessels, both his own and other types encountered during the course of a long voyage. Examples of the non-whaling craft portrayed in the collection include a Baltimore clipper schooner and an auxiliary oceangoing steamship of the 1850s. Though many of these ship portraits may be considered artistically inferior to the work of trained artists, they tend to be technically equal or even superior due to the scrimshanders' firsthand working knowledge of the subject. Such details as the configuration of sails and rigging, the number and placement of whaleboat crewmen, and the particulars of hunting and cutting-in techniques are normally quite accurate. While occasionally whaling vessels were portrayed by marine artists, in some instances the scrimshander's effort is the sole visual depiction of a particular vessel. This is especially true of vessels in service before the advent of photography in the late 1830s.

While the collection includes a tooth with a crude stipple-style engraved portrait of the Provincetown whaling schooner *O. M. Remington*, perhaps the most traditional vessel portrait in the museum is that attributed to a British mariner. In a style reminiscent of a painted work, a beautifully executed broadside view of a full-rigged British merchant ship graces one side of a six-inch-long whale tooth [13]. Adding to the "picture" effect is a frame engraved in a repeat geometric pattern.

Another portrait, this of a whaleship, occupies center stage on a scene engraved the full length of a whale tooth [13]. The inclusion of prominent quarter galleries and the placement of the waist-length figurehead suggest that this vessel may date to the early part of the nineteenth century. Whaleships were frequently second-hand merchant vessels that had outlived their usefulness in the carrying trades and were purchased for the whale fishery. The ship appears to fly the Hawaiian ensign from the mizzen. By the 1850s the number of Hawaiian-flag whaling vessels (many owned and manned by Americans and other foreigners) was growing steadily. They joined American, British, French, and other European whaleships in combing the frigid waters of the Okhotsk and Bering seas for right and bowhead whales, working the lagoons of Baja California for the gray whale, or cruising the tropical sperm whale grounds.

The artistic potential of panbone as a scrimshander's "canvas" is best illustrated by a long rectangular plaque [14] measuring almost eighteen inches wide. A striking panoramic view of an unidentified coastline is boldly engraved for the full width of the piece. A town and large fortification occupy the right side, visually balanced by a whaling bark in the center and a ship-of-the-line and cutter on the left. By placing the bark in the center foreground the scrimshander is intentionally making his vessel the focal point of the scene. The heavy black inking on the white panbone adds measurably to the sense of depth. The depictions of vessels such as the English cutter suggest that this might be the work of a British whaleman.

Of Things Left Behind

. . . at 8 Bells Went on Deck and Stood My Watch had A Very Pleasant Night Talked to My Friend Amos About . . . those Dear Creatures We Left Behind us Which Brought to mind by Gone scenes and kindled in my Bosom A Great Anxiety to Behold the Objects of my Love . . .[6]

14. An unidentified port of call is boldly engraved on this panbone plaque,
17¾ x 4¾ in. (45.1 x 12.1 cm.).
Source: Captain Marion Eppley, 83.487

Gurdon Hall was only eight weeks into what would be a two-year voyage aboard the *Charles Phelps* of Stonington when he scribbled these lines in his journal. The conversation with his shipmate was not unusual, as it focused on one of the prime hardships attendant to pelagic whaling; namely the long separations from home and family, friends and, for many – women. For so many whalemen, women were synonymous with home. Southampton native Francis Cook, a boatsteerer aboard the ship *Sheffield* of Cold Spring Harbor, perhaps summarized it best when, recording a mid-ocean rendezvous with a British vessel, he noted:

The Barque passed very close to us and there were quite a number of Lady passengers. I did not like to look at them but I could not keep my eyes off them. They put me in mind of home. all was Suddenly brought up to my mind in a moment. while gasing on their forms I was transported thousands of miles. I was at home. my friends were around me but another moment dissipated the whole and left nothing but a wild waste of waters before me.[7]

15. The latest fashions as interpreted by the whaleman. At left, *a matched pair of teeth attributed to Manuel Enos, 5⅞ in. (15 cm.); at right, a woman framed by a stylized tree, 7 in. (17.8 cm.).*
Sources: Mrs. Warren A. Beh, 83.300.1–2; Weston Howland, 83.372

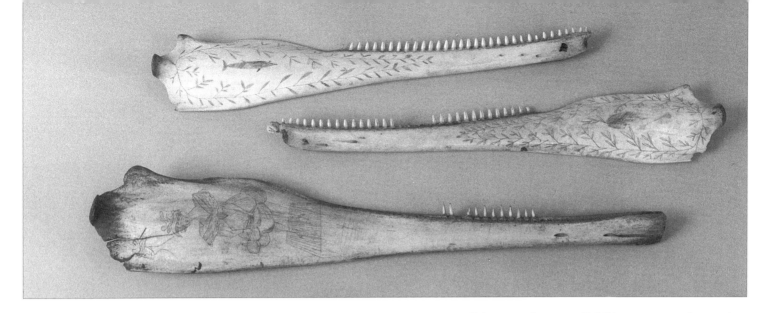

16. Porpoise jaws were engraved in much the same manner as sperm whale jaws. At top, a matched pair include floral imagery and a sketch of a porpoise, 12⅞ in. (32.7 cm.). A fashion portrait occupies the example below, 15⅜ in. (39.1 cm.).
Sources: Mrs. Walter K. Earle, 83.376.1–2; Hoyt Ammidon, 83.386

Statistically, one of the subjects most frequently encountered on scrimshaw is women. In contrast to many other scrimshaw subjects, the vast majority of these portraits were copied directly from printed illustrations using the pin-prick method described in chapter 1. Consequently, they tend to illustrate women dressed in the latest fashions from England or the Continent, suggesting that popular periodicals of the day were the source of many of these designs. *Godey's Lady's Book, Harper's Weekly* and *Harper's New Monthly Magazine, Ballou's Pictorial Drawing Room Companion*; these and other publications are frequently listed as probable image sources, though researchers have had only modest success in matching such portraits with the original illustrations.

But did more than availability prompt the scrimshander to seek out these printed models? Clifford Ashley, the whaleman, artist, and author, held that in general whalemen felt unequal to the task of accurately and stylishly depicting women.[8] The bold patterns characteristic of some of these high-style fashions may have also appealed to the scrimshander's sense of the dramatic, suggesting even wilder or more colorful treatments of the basic design. For example, a pair of teeth in the collection, apparently engraved by the same hand, bear portraits traced from the same image but with different detailing and inking.

The collection is full of such women's portraits, ranging in date from the 1840s to the 1890s. A particularly graceful rendering on a tooth [15] shows a young woman standing under a stylized bowed tree. Like most portraits of this type the figure has been pin-pricked from an illustration, but the supporting design elements have been engraved freehand. Of three porpoise jaws [16] in the museum, each like a miniature version of the sperm

17. *Detail of a porpoise jaw, illustraing a pin-pricked portrait of a dancer. Note practice sketch at upper left. See Figure 16.*

Source: Hoyt Ammidon, 83.386

whale's lower jaw, one bears a full-length woman's portrait [17] similarly traced from a published sketch.

While there are only a handful of attributable scrimshaw examples in the collection, among them are matched pairs of whale teeth and walrus tusks credited to Manuel Enos. The teeth [15], each nearly six inches in length, bear full-length portraits of what appears to be the same woman in different poses. The skilled use of black, red, green, blue, and yellow inks heightens the visual effect. This is work of high quality indeed and has traditionally been attributed to the man they called "Big Manuel."

A Portuguese whaleman recruited in the Azores, Manuel Enos came to Cold Spring Harbor in the 1840s. Although he is commonly thought to have first shipped aboard the ship *Huntsville* in 1849, there is some evidence to suggest that as a teenager he may first have sailed aboard the ship *Sheffield* on her 1845–49 voyage.[9] He definitely served as a boatsteerer aboard the *Sheffield*, 1854–59. A brief stint ashore as a storekeeper proved disastrous, and 1860 found him back whaling as first mate of the bark *Java* of New Bedford. In 1864 he assumed command of the vessel, and it is during an ensuing forty-month-long cruise that he is believed to have engraved a pair of large walrus tusks [18] with pin-pricked women's portraits. One of the tusks features a woman and young girl standing together [19]. The woman, who holds a sheet of paper engraved "Java/Capt. Enos," is believed to represent Enos's wife Susan, and the girl their daughter Melva.[10] The twenty-eight-inch-long tusks have been intentionally stained and bear a lustrous golden brown pátina. Sadly, upon arriving back in Cold Spring Harbor Enos learned that Melva had died during his absence at sea.

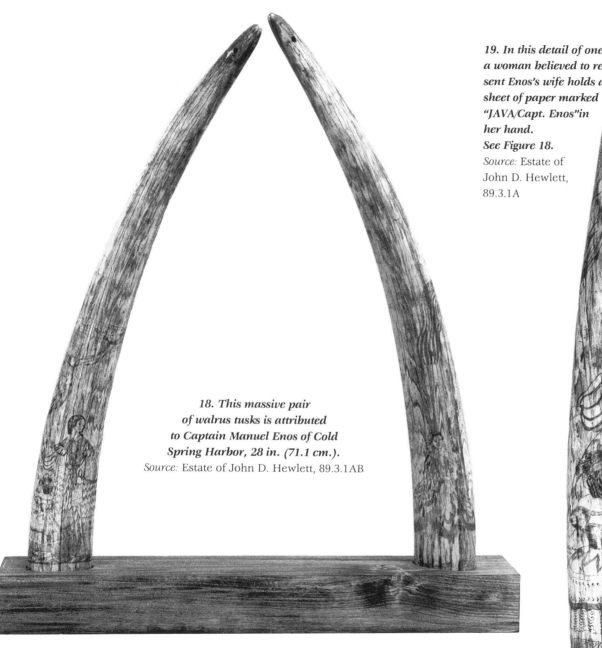

19. In this detail of one tusk a woman believed to represent Enos's wife holds a sheet of paper marked "JAVA/Capt. Enos"in her hand.
See Figure 18.
Source: Estate of John D. Hewlett, 89.3.1A

18. This massive pair of walrus tusks is attributed to Captain Manuel Enos of Cold Spring Harbor, 28 in. (71.1 cm.).
Source: Estate of John D. Hewlett, 89.3.1AB

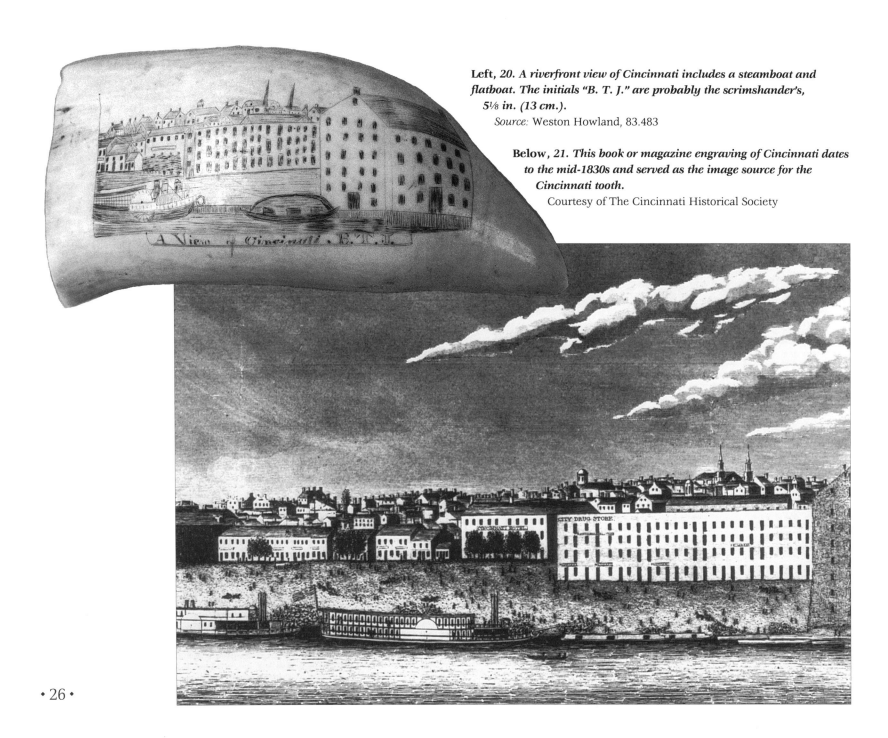

Left, 20. *A riverfront view of Cincinnati includes a steamboat and flatboat. The initials "B. T. J." are probably the scrimshander's,* 5⅛ in. (13 cm.).
Source: Weston Howland, 83.483

Below, 21. *This book or magazine engraving of Cincinnati dates to the mid-1830s and served as the image source for the Cincinnati tooth.*
Courtesy of The Cincinnati Historical Society

Am Thinking About, Home, all the time.[11]

An unidentified crewman aboard the bark *Alice* of Cold Spring Harbor made this admission while the vessel was drifting among ice floes in the frigid Okhotsk Sea. If the surviving journals of whalemen are any indication, then thoughts of home and family were constantly on the minds of these men as they labored in waters as distant as the Bering Sea or the Indian Ocean.

Images of home vary widely, each reflecting the memories of the scrimshander. Some, like a freehand rendering of Boston's Minot's Ledge Lighthouse found on a tooth, have obvious maritime connections. Others, such as a tooth bearing "A View of Cincinnati" [20], remind us that not every whaleman was born within spitting distance of salt water. Farm boys from Ohio, Pennsylvania, upstate New York, and elsewhere found themselves serving alongside men to whom the sea was as familiar as the land. It is uncertain whether "B. T. J.," the engraver of the Cincinnati tooth, was from the Queen City, or even from Ohio, for the source of this scene is a circa 1835 engraving from an unidentified book or periodical [21].

This day my Dear M is 25 years old if She is living.[12]

Captain Edwin P. Brown of the Greenport whaleship *Lucy Ann* wrote this poignant line in his journal nearly two years into an 1844–47 voyage to the North Pacific. "Dear M" was his wife Martha, whom he married shortly before sailing. Such sentiments were undoubtedly reflected in the work of scrimshanders. Some examples depict what might be the whaleman's home town. Other pieces carry a stronger domestic message. For example, a baleen corset busk horizontally engraved with multiple vignettes includes not only an engraving of what is probably the scrimshander's own house, but also a scene showing a sleeping chamber complete with canopied bed and candle stand [22].

The long periods of separation left many whalemen fearful of what they would find upon homecoming. Captain Brown's marking of his wife's twenty-fifth birthday is

22. A homesick whaleman included a bedchamber among the images on a baleen busk.
Source: Weston Howland, 83.553

tempered by a gnawing uncertainty about her well-being. As Captain Enos learned upon his return to Cold Spring Harbor in 1869, such fears were not unfounded. In an age of high mortality among children and adults alike, Enos's experience was not uncommon. Bad news from home could prompt the inclusion of such popular mourning imagery as funeral urns, weeping willows – even memorial monuments [23] – on a piece of scrimshaw.

> good by old Montauk the next time that you are in
> sight our hearts will leap for joy and our breasts filled
> with hope joy and fear.[13]

Long Islander Francis Cook reflected on his departure from home as the Cold Spring Harbor whaleship *Sheffield* cleared that familiar point of land and sailed southeast into the Atlantic. Already he and many of his mates were looking ahead to the day when Montauk Point and its landmark beacon would welcome them back to more familiar waters.

Another, as yet unidentified, Long Island whaleman obviously shared this sentiment and literally went to great lengths in its expression. On a strip of baleen [24] approaching seven feet in length he patiently engraved a birdseye view of what seems to be part of Long Island Sound along with Gardiners and Peconic Bays. By a technique best described as "selective compression" the scrimshander has placed highly detailed vignettes of one or more Long Island coastal villages and shipping along the length of the piece. Full-rigged ships, barks, schooners, sloops, and steamboats are scattered about the harbors, rivers, and bays of this superb rendering. The designs of the steamboats suggest a probable date in the 1830s or early 1840s. Many of the domestic, public, and commercial

• 28 •

23. *Among popular mourning images was the tomb or memorial monument. This example is included on a panbone busk. See Figure 28.*
Source: Weston Howland, 83.320

25. *This highly detailed vignette, believed to be one of eastern Long Island's whaling ports, is included on the strip of baleen. See Figure 24.*
Source: Museum Purchase, 90.5

structures in the villages [25] are so detailed as to suggest that the artist may have had specific locales in mind, like Sag Harbor or Greenport. Engraved decorative strips of baleen, especially of such large size, are not very common. As will be seen in chapter 4, this flexible material found much wider use in functional scrimshaw items such as corset busks and ditty boxes.

24. A cartographic masterpiece: a map of eastern Long Island engraved on a long strip of baleen, 69½ in. (176.5 cm.).
Source: Museum Purchase, 90.5. Photograph by Mary Anne Stets

Of Symbolism and Other Themes

Whalemen carried to sea with them many of the attitudes and beliefs held by their countrymen ashore. The spirit of nationalism that pervaded American society, particularly in the first half of the nineteenth century, frequently found expression in the work of the shipboard artist. Such feelings were often delineated in the form of one or more popular patriotic icons. The elevation of George Washington to demigod status, for example, insured his presence on decorative scrimshaw of all types, including a late-nineteenth-century tooth in this collection.

Nearly as popular a human image is the allegorical figure of Liberty. In many of the depictions of this character she wears a liberty cap, the symbol of freedom popularized during the French Revolution. Undoubtedly the finest rendering of Liberty in the museum is a wonderfully conceived freehand portrait on a tooth [26] in which the figure holds an outstretched American flag above her head. Although the identity of the hero whose bust rests on a pedestal by her side remains a mystery, the portrait of an auxiliary steamship on the reverse suggests that the piece dates to the 1840s or 1850s. Complementing this portrait is a pin-pricked image of the goddess of Justice engraved on a tooth, and a late-nineteenth-century rendering of the Statue of Liberty that graces a large walrus tusk.

In terms of sheer numbers, however, the American eagle is undoubtedly the single most popular patriotic motif to be found on either decorative or functional scrimshaw items. Whether boldly engraved from memory or carefully pin-pricked from an illustration, this feathered symbol of American freedom and strength turns up everywhere. The eagle appears by itself, as on one tooth [26], or more commonly as part of a grouping of other, frequently unrelated, subjects on decorative and utilitarian objects alike.

Patriotism was often expressed by whalemen in their depictions of American naval vessels of the day. While none of the purely decorative pieces in this collection bear such images, several of the functional items detailed in chapter 4 incorporate this theme. In the decades following the War of 1812 the theme of American

26. A patriotic pairing of teeth matches Liberty, 6⅝ in. (16.8 cm.), and the American eagle, 4⅜ in. (11.1 cm.).
Sources: Weston Howland, 83.309; Sherburn Sweetland, 83.522

naval glory gained in popularity among American seamen who remembered both the arrogance of the Royal Navy and its threat to the twin foundations of the mariner's livelihood – "Free Trade and Sailors' Rights." A series of signal victories scored by the republic's young navy against this powerful force, captured in words and – more importantly – images in magazines or books like *The Naval Monument* (1816) provided plenty of grist for the scrimshander. By the time of the Civil War, however, the hallowed tradition of Britain bashing had largely given way to interest in more contemporary naval events.

An interest in nature is quite evident in a great deal of scrimshaw work. Long absence from familiar natural scenes may have contributed to the popularity of potted plants, flowers, and trees that appear on so many pieces. A tooth [27] engraved with a simple but elegant floral arrangement in a pot or vase typifies this motif, which also appears with great regularity on corset busks. Stylized natural designs like this may also be related to the ancient Tree of Life motif that was so popular in England and America in the eighteenth and early-nineteenth centuries.[14] Perhaps more widespread, though, is the use of branches, vine-work, or leaf-and-tendril patterns as decorative borders on all manner of scrimshaw. Fauna, particularly birds, also come in for their share of attention at the hands of the scrimshander.

For the globe-girdling whaleman an interest in the exotic was often a result of firsthand experience. Depictions of foreign places and peoples are occasionally found, like the portraits of Pacific islanders noted on a pair of teeth in the collection.

Not to be overlooked are other topics of apparent interest to whalemen (not all of which are represented in the collection), among them religious and Masonic themes

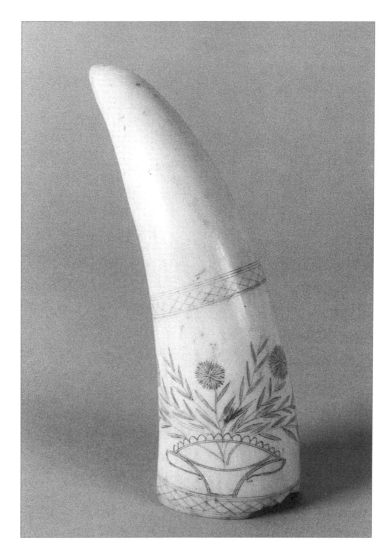

27. The ancient Tree of Life design inspired this floral rendering on a tooth, 4 in. (10.2 cm.).
Source: Weston Howland, 83.490

and sentimentality. Add to this a mild fixation with literary characters, not the least of which are seafaring types like the female buccaneers Fanny Campbell or Alwilda, and one can begin to sense the variety of iconographic avenues explored by the whaleman.

In looking at the renderings of the varied themes that caught and held the fancy of the whaleman it is clear that there is a common denominator: geometric designs. Such patterns, either by themselves or repeated in linear fashion, inject a vigor and originality to even a slavishly pin-pricked design. Geometric motifs provide floors, walls, and ceilings for human figures, frames for vessel portraits, dividers for multiple vignettes, clothing patterns for fashionable women, and decorative borders for a bewildering variety of other visual subjects. While a review of the illustrations in this chapter alone can suggest the variety and frequency of geometric patterns, an examination of utilitarian scrimshaw items in chapter 4 will only reemphasize the significance of such designs.

4

"Ingenious Contrivances" The Whaleman as Craftsman

Almost All hands employed in getting out Busks
swifts fids gimlet handles canes and sutch like scrimshonting
to present their friends with when we get holm.[1]

Whaleman Gurdon Hall's passing observation points up the fact that in terms of variety – if not sheer quantity – functional items were at least as important to the scrimshander as engraved teeth, tusks, and panbone. A bewildering range of useful objects was produced by the hands of whalemen and other mariners; but it is misleading to consider such creations as strictly utilitarian in nature. For many of these pieces incorporate a marvelous degree of aesthetic content in their design, construction, and ornamentation. The strength of the museum's scrimshaw collection clearly rests on these functional forms, with their wonderful melding of artistry and craftsmanship.

With an Eye to Fashion

Clothing styles exerted a great influence on the design of certain scrimshaw items. Thin ribs of panbone or baleen had been an integral part of women's corsets from at least the eighteenth century. In such items of apparel a wider stay was inserted in a pocket in the front of the corset. Ranging in length from perhaps twelve to fourteen inches, these thin "corset boards" or busks were frequently made of wood, and there are surviving examples with marvelous carving on them.

Whalemen were able to utilize two different materials, panbone and baleen, in fashioning these gift items for a loved one. Once shaped to the desired size any number of decorative designs could be engraved, either vertically or horizontally. Frequently these designs were set off as separate vignettes by the use of geometric or vine-work borders. Sailing home to Stonington, Connecticut, aboard the ship *Charles Phelps*, Gurdon Hall helped a less talented shipmate in such a task, as noted in his journal: "Spent my Watch Below in Scrimpshonting a Corset Board for Friend Amos."[2]

The dozens of busks found in the collection incorporate a dazzling variety of subjects, some familiar and

some unusual. One thirteen-inch-long panbone example [28] sports familiar vignettes that symbolize life ashore and life at sea. Of special note is the inclusion of a memorial monument, perhaps in memory of a loved one who died while the whaleman was at sea. Mixed in with the domestic and marine imagery is a hot-air balloon. Balloon ascensions were exciting highlights of special celebrations at home and were occasionally included on busks. A double lobed or "bifurcated" top enhances the effort while the elaborate repeat sawtooth border frames each vignette in a crisp manner.

In contrast to many busks that emphasize geometric shapes or inanimate objects, human figures abound on another panbone example [28]. Men, women, and even a child with his dog compete for attention on this boldly inked busk. The lobed top has been engraved with double crescent moons over a portrait of the whaleman's vessel and what might be a self portrait and one of his wife.

Geometry and a dash of patriotism characterize a panbone busk with a bevelled top [28]. A multiple star-rosette design at the center and the sentimental "lover's knot" motif near the bottom testify to the scrimshander's competence with scribing compass. Natural imagery abounds in the form of two versions of the ancient Tree of Life motif, one growing in the ground and the other depicted growing in a pot. Of eastern origin, these designs were pop-

28. Panbone busks bore a variety of shapes and imagery. From left, a busk that features images of land, sea, and air, 13⅛ in. (33.3 cm.); human figures dominate a straight edged example, 13¼ in. (33.7 cm.); geometry triumphs on a busk initialed "C. M. P.," 13⅛ in. (33.3 cm.); a red inked heart highlights a shorter example, 11 in. (27.9 cm.).
Sources: Weston Howland, 83.320, 83.530, 83.531; Stanley C. Walters, 83.212

ular in Britain and found their way to New England as design elements in English trade goods.[3] Though we do not know if the initials "C. M. P." at the bottom refer to the maker or the intended recipient, the lone American eagle with shield and flag makes the scrimshander's nationality clear. A strikingly similar busk in the Sag Harbor Whaling Museum collection may be by the same hand.

Slightly shorter at eleven inches in length, a fourth example of a panbone busk [28] makes bold use of one of the most prevalent and important folk motifs, the heart.[4] A heart, shaded in red, symbolizes the scrimshander's feeling for the recipient, who would literally wear it close to her own heart. While the accompanying star-in-circle and bird motifs are not uncommon elements, the inclusion of a thistle suggests that the scrimshander may have been a Scot, many of whom served in both the American and British whaling fleets. Green-blue inking highlights this floral design.

Baleen's potential was not overlooked in fashioning busks. One Joseph Williams of New Bedford engraved such a piece [29] in 1848, signing his name [30] along one of the sawtooth border elements on the busk. Unfortunately, in 1848 there were at least five whalemen by this name serving aboard New Bedford vessels; thus it has not been possible to attribute the piece to one specific individual. It is possible,

Left, 29. A trio of baleen busks. **From left,** *a signed example by Joseph Williams, 12¼ in. (31.1 cm.); a masterpiece of geometry and folk designs initialed "C K/D K," 13⅞ in. (35.3 cm.); a wide example affords space for samples of both naval and public architecture, 13¼ in. (33.7 cm).*
Sources: Weston Howland, 83.470; Mrs. Theodore F. Humphrey, 83.472; Weston Howland, 83.471

Right, 30. *Detail of the Joseph Williams busk. See Figure 29.*
Source: Weston Howland, 83.470

however, that the inclusion of the initials "N B" near the signature might actually indicate the New Bedford whaleship *New Bedford*, aboard which one Joseph Williams served as blacksmith during an 1846–49 voyage.[5] Williams's engraving efforts, characteristic of so many other busk makers, were predominantly geometric in form.

Occasionally busks were engraved in a horizontal fashion. One, bearing the initials "C K" and "D K" [29], is a virtuoso performance of compass skill. A combination of star-rosettes, ellipses, heart, lozenge, and stylized lover's knot designs are executed along its length. A two-masted schooner included in the array serves as a reminder of the busk's nautical origins.

The nearly two-inch width of a third baleen busk [29] provides plenty of room for an elaborate architectural rendering of a large Greek Revival-style church or public building. The scrimshander's pride in the country's navy is also represented in a fine depiction of an American frigate at anchor. Completing the design is another Tree of Life motif, along with various geometric border patterns. It is uncertain whether the initials "A H" engraved on the reverse refer to the scrimshander.

If the corset busk was a labor of love for another, then the cane was thus for the whaleman himself. Perhaps the most telling comment about canes was that recorded by a bored crewman aboard the ship *Clifford Wayne* in 1844: "Nothing to do but make canes to support our dignity when we are home."[6] Canes were an important part of a man's wardrobe and, judging by the many whaling journal references and surviving examples, shipboard production must have been prodigious.

Wilson Andrews aboard the ship *Hibernia* noted that he was "employed in making canes of all kinds"[7]; while a bored Henry Rogers on board of the *New England* simply

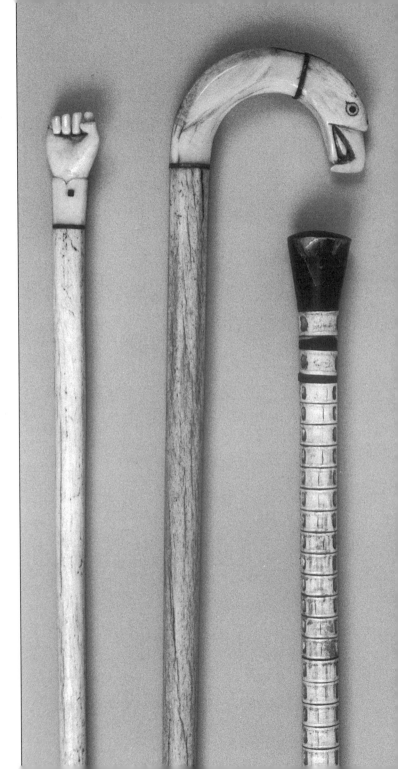

stated "i am Employed in Making canes."[8] As usual, Gurdon Hall had something to say about this subject when he wrote that "Capt H[all] is Buisy makeing and Ivory Cane for Himself. guess it will look pretty fair when finished."[9]

The collection boasts over two dozen scrimshaw canes, incorporating various combinations of ivory, panbone, baleen, wood, metal, shell, and other secondary materials. As varied as the materials are the designs, which include geometric turnings, heads and assorted body parts, animals, and other shapes.

The fist motif is found on functional items as diverse as bodkins, swifts, and pie crimpers. A small, twenty-seven-inch-long panbone cane [31], possibly intended as a lady's walking stick, bears this same design carved in ivory with baleen accents. Among the sometimes contradictory theories surrounding the fist design are that it symbolizes: the giving of a gift, the method of holding an object, or the pent-up aggression resulting from long periods of shipboard isolation. Heavy panbone canes that could be useful in a brawl might support

31. Cane handles incorporated a wide variety of shapes and materials. The third example is formed of shark vertebrae with a horn handle.
Sources: Weston Howland, 83.529; Anonymous, 83.528; Rodney W. Williams, 83.494; Weston Howland, 83.495

the latter theory, but this particular example is much too delicate in its proportions to be of any such use.

A heftier cane is a panbone example with a curved ivory handle carved in the shape of an eagle's head [31]. The eyes are inlaid with baleen, and two thin spacers of this same material help define the handle, which also boasts a diamond-shape inlay of colorful abalone.

While mariners have traditionally feared sharks as indiscriminate killing machines, whalemen in particular had reason to cast a jaundiced eye on these predators. The bloody business of killing and cutting-in whales frequently attracted sharks who gorged themselves on the whale carcass, thus reducing the yield of oil for the whalemen. In addition, the appalling prospect of falling overboard into bloodied water was a nightmare for officers and foremast hands alike. Yet, bored whalemen occasionally lured sharks with large baited hooks, and took some glee in killing them. If a whale tooth was a kind of trophy of the whaling business, then perhaps a shark vertebrae cane could be considered a symbol of triumph over this enemy. With a metal rod as a core a cane could be fashioned from the cartilaginous backbone. One straight-neck example [31] measures nearly thirty-six inches and is equipped with a flared handle made of segments of horn.

Although some scrimshanders had access to lathes on shipboard, much of the turning work found on utilitarian items was the result of careful use of files and saws. One of the finest examples of such work in the museum is a very heavy panbone cane [31] that features a combination of rope twist turning and vertical fluting separated by a finely woven and applied band of baleen. A hole drilled through the shaft near the top is plugged with inlays of silver while the turned whale-ivory handle is separated from the shaft by a thin, scalloped-edge disk of horn or baleen.

In most cases the identity of a cane's maker is lost as time passes. One scrimshander, however, avoided anonymity by engraving both his name and the date of his work on the bulbous whale-ivory handle [32]. Although we do not know the complete identity of "C. King" we can appreciate the straightforward style and competence of his execution in making this cane [33] with its turned and tapered panbone shaft.

A particular boldness of design characterizes a curved-handled example [33] in the museum. The tapered octagonal panbone shaft leads to a handle comprised of alternating bands of whale ivory and a dark tropical hard-

Below, 32. C. King engraved his name and date on the whale ivory handle of his cane. See Figure 33.
Source: Weston Howland, 83.4

Left, 33. Wood was frequently used for shafts or decorative inlay in canes.
Sources: Weston Howland, 83.4, 83.317, 83.316; Anonymous, 83.356

wood. A similar hardwood serves as the shaft for a cane [33] with a superbly turned whale-ivory handle. Incised grooves on the head have been filled with red and black sealing wax, thus creating a contrasting color effect that highlights its bulbous shape.

Like the clenched fist motif, carved examples of a woman's leg have been linked to emotions created by the stress of shipboard isolation. Whether such a design is truly the result of repressed sexual feelings or simply a "naughty" gesture will have to be debated elsewhere. The collection does include a panbone cane [33] with a whale-ivory handle carved in this very shape. The engraved boot is separated from the exposed knee by thin bands of metal and baleen or horn, and a thicker disk of baleen links the handle and shaft.

Miscellaneous clothing accessories [34] are also found in the scrimshaw collection, among them an ivory and tortoiseshell watch chain and several pairs of cufflinks. One pair, carved from whale ivory, are pleasing in their simplicity. Another set, credited to the hands of whaleman Samuel Mitchell [35], combines one-inch-diameter disks of tortoiseshell with whale ivory to good effect. Mitchell, whose better-known brother, West, was a whaling master,

Lower right, 34. *Clothing accessories and jewelry include whale ivory cufflinks, ⅞ x ⅝ in. (2.3 x 1.6 cm.); tortoiseshell cufflinks attributed to Samuel Mitchell, 1 in. (2.5 cm.); tortoiseshell and ivory brooch attributed to Jesse T. Sherman, 2¾ in. (7 cm.); whale ivory pinky ring, ⅞ in. (2.3 cm.); and whale ivory scarf ring, 1¼ in. (3.2 cm.).*
Sources: Anonymous, 83.513.14; Mary J. Holmes, 83.544.1–2; Anonymous, 83.377, 83.513.5; Weston Howland, 83.232

Upper right, 35. *Daguerreotype of whaleman Samuel Mitchell of Cold Spring Harbor.*
Source: Mary J. Holmes, 77.48.1

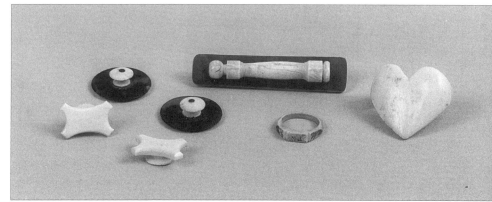

was himself mate of several whalers, including the bark *Thomas Dickason* of New Bedford, 1869–71.[10] He moved to Cold Spring Harbor in 1861 and seems to have divided his time between whaling and commanding schooners in the coasting trade.[11]

Among the scarf rings in the collection is one [34] carved from whale ivory in the shape of a heart. In both size and function it contrasts with a delicate finger ring [34] whose flat top face is engraved with a leaf and berry design flanked by a red wax-inlaid heart and the initials "H. W." Like the tortoiseshell cufflinks, a whale-ivory and tortoiseshell brooch [34] bears an attribution. The 2¾-inch-long piece is credited to the hand of Jesse T. Sherman, who was master of the whaleship *James Arnold* of New Bedford in the 1880s.

Of Stitches and Seams

Sewing accessories compose another major category of utilitarian objects fashioned by scrimshanders. Despite the growth of clothing manufacturing in the nineteenth century a great deal of sewing work was done in the home. New England in particular boasted a vigorous home textile industry into the 1830s, and thus scrimshanders produced items that they remembered from home. These ranged from the simplest bodkin to the most elaborate winding swift, each to the delight of the recipients.

Simple items like knitting needles were produced in some quantity. The collection includes a pair crafted of panbone with acorn-shaped finials. Also characteristic of relatively simple sewing tools are the many different bodkins [36], whose mundane use in piercing cloth frequently stands in stark contrast to their design and degree of ornamentation. Carved from panbone, whale ivory, or walrus

ivory these small sewing aides often incorporated symbolic imagery like hearts or hands, or even inlays of colored wax, mother-of-pearl, or tortoiseshell. In a pinch, some of these could also double as decorative hair ornaments.

If bodkins and knitting needles represent the more basic sewing items to be crafted by the whaleman, then surely the winding swift must rank as the most elaborate. Designed to hold a skein of yarn when extra hands were not available, these collapsible basket-like reels or cages were perhaps the supreme challenge for the experienced scrimshander. With long panbone shafts and stays, whale- or walrus-ivory cups or finials, bases, and locking clamps, and frequent use of contrasting inlays, swifts were among the most complex products ever crafted on shipboard. The necessity for considerable tool experience, plus the requirement for a protected spot to fabricate and assemble the pieces, suggests that swifts were probably most frequently made by skilled crewmen like coopers or carpenters, or ships' officers whose accommodations were more spacious and secure than those of foremast hands.[12]

While some swifts were designed to stand atop a table or decorative base, the majority seem to have been intended to clamp to the edge of a table or arm of a chair using a locking thumbscrew. Most of the swifts in the collection utilize the latter arrangement, including one

36. Bodkins in all shapes and sizes. **From left, *whale ivory with tortoiseshell inlay, 2⅞ in. (7.4 cm.); panbone with hearts, 3½ in. (8.9 cm.); whale ivory fist with red wax buttons, 3⅞ in. (9.8 cm.); whale ivory with open handle, 5 in. (12.7 cm.); whale ivory with red wax and abalone inlay, 4¼ in. (10.8 cm.); walrus ivory with bulbous finial, 3½ in. (8.9 cm.); whale ivory with columns, 3⅝ in. (9.2 cm.).***
Source: Weston Howland, 83.460.32,36,44,54,42,34,43

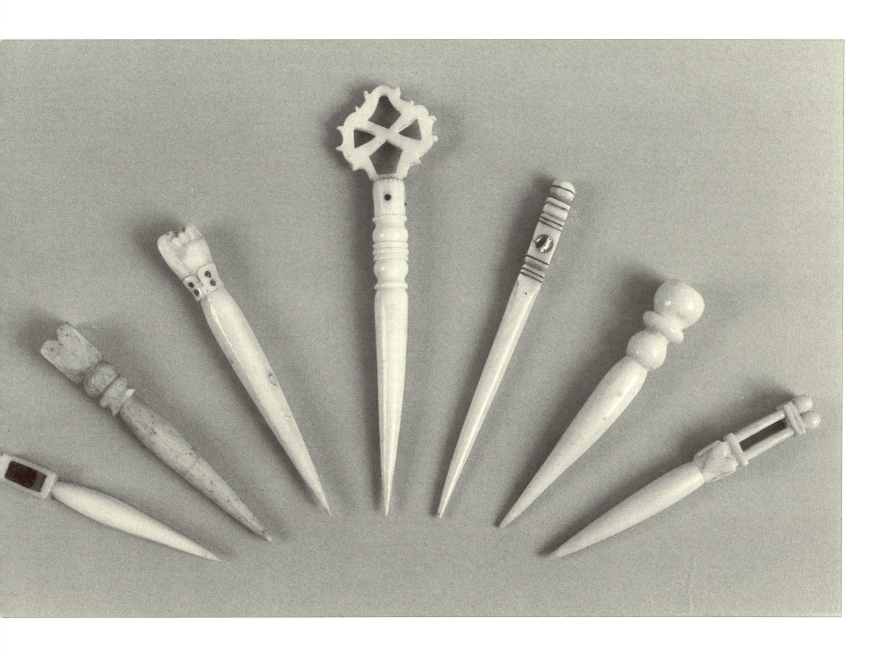

example [37] that incorporates a sawtooth banding of tortoiseshell around the sliding shaft lock. Although the basic umbrella-like operation of the cage is common to all swifts, scrimshanders created a wonderful variety of shapes and designs for the base clamps. Details of several other swifts in the collection [38] suggest the range of possibilities. One swift has a turned and scribed whale-ivory clamp in the shape of a barrel and includes colored sealing wax for contrast. The other features a rectangular whale-ivory clamp inlaid with tortoiseshell and mother-of-pearl in such shapes as stars, lozenges, circles, hearts, and rectangles.

Work with needle and thread required other types of tools, and scrimshanders were willing to oblige. Among these specialized items were needle holders, small ivory or panbone devices with one or more narrow slots designed to hold sewing needles while not in use. Recently, it has been suggested that such holders may actually be "knitting sheaths," devices that allowed a woman to knit while walking. She would place one of a pair of special, very fine knitting needles in the slot while she held and manipulated the other.[13] In either application the piece was designed to be stitched to clothing.

Many of the needle holders (or "knitting sheaths?") in the collection incorporate a variation of the heart motif known as the "asymetrical heart." Common as a folk image in northern New England, it also has religious overtones in the form of the "bleeding heart" popular among Catholic French-Canadians.[14] Three of the four specimens illustrated [39] include this shape. One example is also pierced with two five-point stars as well as that ancient folk art element, the fylfot. Symbolic of good luck, the propeller-like fylfot is also refered to as the "whirling sun."[15]

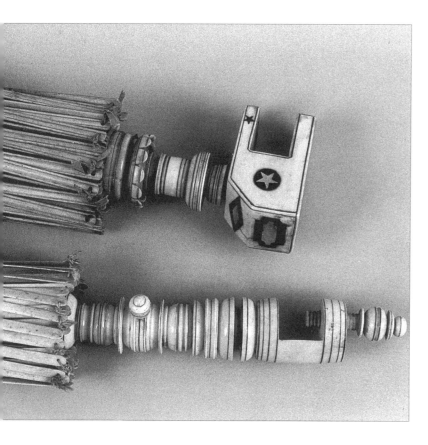

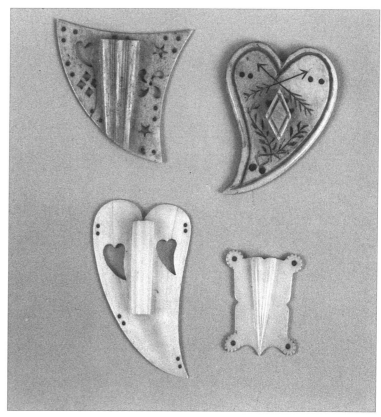

Below, 39. *Hearts abound on these delicate whale ivory needle holders. Clockwise from upper left: diamonds, heart, fylfot, and stars cover one pierced example, 1¾ in. (4.5 cm.); a holder in the shape of an asymetrical heart includes red wax inlay, 1⅞ in. (4.8 cm.); a non-heart shape specimen, 1⅛ in. (2.8 cm); another asymetrical heart shape pierced by a pair of similar hearts, 2⅛ in. (5.4 cm.).*
Source: Anonymous, 83.513.12,13,8,10

Left, 37. *Like many swifts this example is topped by a turned ivory cup designed to support a ball of yarn. Tortoiseshell inlay in a sawtooth pattern adds a graceful accent to the swift, 20¼ in. (51.5 cm.).*
Source: Weston Howland, 83.526

Above, 38. *Most swifts were designed to clamp on the arm of a chair or edge of a table. Base clamps sometimes featured elaborate inlay work (top) or turnings (bottom).*
Sources: Mrs. Warren A. Beh, 83.208; Mrs. Henry D. Bixby, 83.480

40. Painstaking inlay work and a carved ivory dove highlight this sewing stand, 10 in. (25.4 cm.).
Source: Weston Howland, 83.581

41. Asymetrical or "bleeding" hearts pierce the sides of this coin silver-inlaid ivory basket, 6¾ in. (17.2 cm.).
Source: Weston Howland, 83.378

Storage of thread required such basic implements as spools, and the collection contains several examples made of panbone or ivory. More elaborate, and worthy of an experienced scrimshander, was the multi-tiered sewing stand. An octagonal example in the museum [40] features two tiers for the storage of both tall and short spools. Contrasting light and dark woods and wood inlay complement the whale-ivory feet, knobs, and spool holders. While many such stands are topped by pincushions this example is surmounted by a dove carved from whale ivory.

The safe storage of small sewing or household items at home or even on shipboard encouraged the creation of various open or closed containers. A superb example of the former is a hexagonal whale-ivory basket [41] affixed to a scalloped wood and ivory base. Cotton twine links the sides, each of which is pierced with a crescent and a pair of asymetrical hearts. The ivory base is inlaid with a silver disk in the center and partial disks at each angle. Completing the bold design are six inlaid strips of baleen radiating from the center disk.

"Spent All my Watch Below Scrimpshonting A Black Bone Box."[16]

With this brief remark Gurdon Hall, the irrepressible journalist and scrimshander aboard the whaleship *Charles Phelps*, noted the construction of another functional sewing aid. Covered boxes of baleen (Hall's "Black Bone") and panbone also served well for safe storage of sewing or domestic items. Flexible strips of baleen,

42. An American eagle and fortification grace one side of a round baleen box, diam. 8½ in. (21.6 cm.).
Source: Weston Howland, 83.512

engraved, steamed and bent around circular, oval, or elliptical wood bases, created boxes of wondrous delicacy and grace. As with busks scrimshanders used a variety of imagery in the decoration of these functional items. A round example [42] includes an American eagle perched over a military fortification on one side and an American ship-of-the-line [43] on the other. The baleen-covered wooden lid is engraved with an elaborate geometric design featuring checkerboard, crescent, sawtooth, and rope-work motifs as well as vine-work patterns.

43. A scrimshander's pride in his country's navy is evident in this detailed sketch of an American warship on a baleen box. See Figure 42.
Source: Weston Howland, 83.512

The relatively large surfaces of these sewing or ditty boxes enabled the execution of large or complicated designs. Another of these baleen examples, elliptical in shape, emphasizes several architectural designs of both domestic and foreign origin. The simplicity of a Greek Revival-style New England church [44] on one side of the box stands in stark contrast to the elaborately detailed Moorish palace [45] found on the opposite face. A bold geometric element in the form of a checkerboard bottom border provides a visual link between the dissimilar structures. The church may have been engraved freehand, but it is likely that the palace was copied from a published illustration rather than sketched from life.

The elegance and simplicity of design found in many boxes is evident even without the addition of engraved decoration. A perfect example of this is an oval box [46] whose thin panbone sides lack any ornamentation save graceful riveted joint laps or "fingers." The contrast between the white bone sides and the dark wooden lid provides a crispness of design that enhances the total visual effect of the piece.

44. An oval baleen box includes domestic church architecture on one side. Note the "finger" joints that bind the side, 6¾ x 5½ in. (17.2 x 14 cm.).
Source: Mrs. E. Sanderson Cushman, 83.333

Matters of Taste

If the various sewing aids wrought by scrimshanders were of genuine help to wives and sweethearts at home, then equally so could be cooking and dining implements created in off duty hours. Proof of this fact abounds in scrimshaw collections around the country where food preparation, serving, and dining utensils can be found in great number and variety.

Some of these functional scrimshaw objects are simple and straightforward, like a scoop fashioned from a coconut shell [46]. Useful for scooping bulk

A popular kitchen item much favored by whalemen and others was the rolling pin. After all, its use almost always foretold good eating ahead. Whalemen with access to lathes were especially liable to produce such utensils. Though all-panbone examples exist, more commonly rolling pins were fashioned of hardwood with decorative end caps or handles of panbone or ivory. Of the examples found in the collection, one is of very simple design [47], consisting of a thick, tapering hardwood pin with tapered whale-ivory caps. Thin rings of baleen between the roller and the handles provide a visual transition between the elements.

At nearly twenty-two inches in length, a somewhat more elaborate specimen [47] features both a thinner pin and a true handle design. Turned whale ivory sets off the tapered handles from the pin and also serves to cap the handles. Though decorative, such items undoubtedly were used, to their makers' delight.

If scrimshaw scoops were a help in handling flour and other dry commodities, then dippers could be of similar use with water and other liquids. The half dozen dippers in the collection all feature coconut shells for the bowls, but from there the talents and imagination of the individual scrimshander take off. Several of these examples are worth a closer look.

With a carved wooden "monkey tail" handle, one such dipper [48] features a very graceful shape indeed. This is one of at least two dippers in New York collections (the other is at South Street Seaport Museum) that incor-

47. Rolling pins frequently included ivory handles. Top, *a short* **example includes baleen in its construction, 13½ in. (34.3 cm.);** **bottom,** *whale ivory and wood are the sole materials,* **21⅞ in.** **(55.6 cm.).**
Sources: Mary J. Holmes, 83.486; Weston Howland, 83.374

foodstuffs like flour, sugar, and beans, the simple shape is complemented by a turned wooden handle. One wonders whether this might have been part of a set of food handling equipment such as coconut shell bowls, cups, etc. Whalemen came by such shells naturally, as edible coconuts were frequently purchased or collected at islands around the world. For example, sailmaker Frederick Crapser of the Fall River bark *Pantheon* noted "All hands Eating Coconutts and Skrimshoning"[17] while the vessel cruised Pacific waters.

porate an applied overlay of a pewter-color metal on the outside of the bowl. The overlapping circular design emphasizes the roundness of the shell bowl. Though other details of the overall design vary, the similarity of the metal overlay suggests that these are products of the same hand.

One of the largest dippers in the collection [48],

48. A trio of coconut shell dippers: an example with curved "monkey tail" handle and metal overlay, 14¾ in. (37.5 cm.); a dipper with a composite ivory and wood handle, 16¾ in. (42.5 cm.); a miniature specimen with three-piece whale ivory handle, 9 in. (22.9 cm.).

Source: Weston Howland, 83.334, 83.476, 83.466

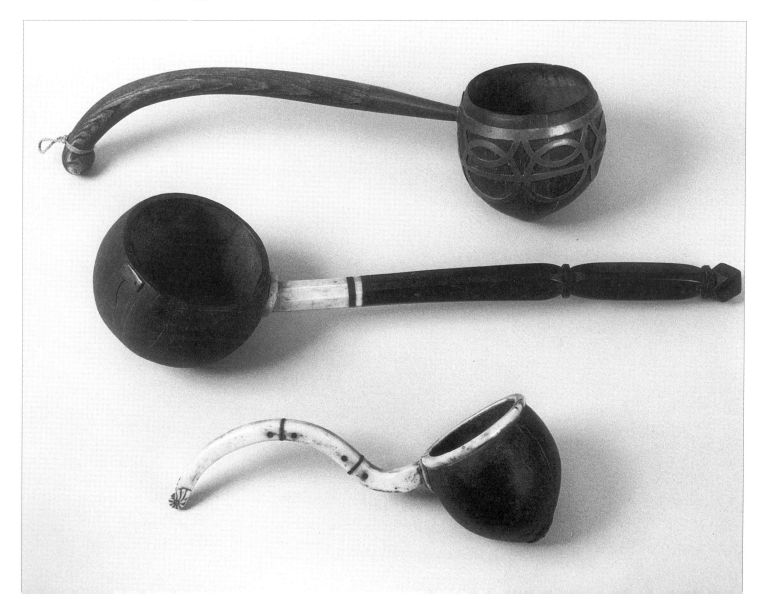

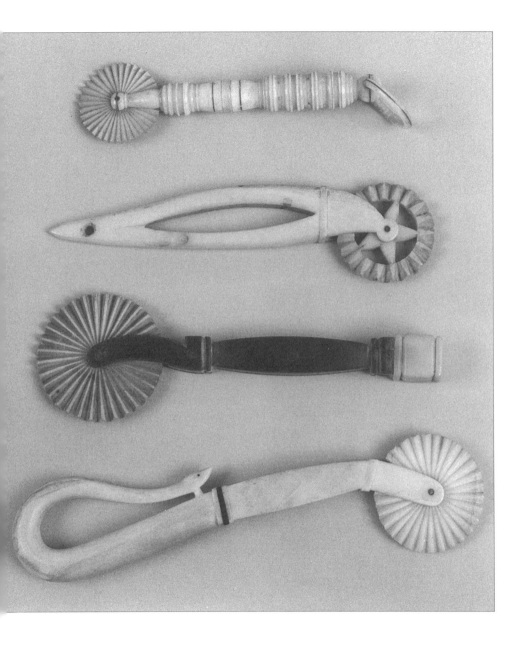

measuring nearly seventeen inches in length, makes good use of whale ivory in its construction. A straight wooden handle, square with beveled edges and ending in a polyhedron or "faceted cube," is linked to the bowl by a similarly shaped whale-ivory segment. A thin segment of hardwood affords additional decoration. As with many dippers, the ivory bracket that attaches handle to bowl is carved in the shape of a heart.

In stark contrast stands the smallest dipper in the Cold Spring Harbor collection [48]. At nine inches long, its size and delicacy of construction makes this more likely a gift to be treasured than used. Pleasing contrast to the coconut bowl is provided by the thin ring of whale ivory applied to the lip. The sharp curve of the segmented whale-ivory handle recalls a pipe stem more than a grip. Though small, the dipper does not lack pleasing details, including the use of tortoiseshell spacers between handle segments, a heart-shape mounting bracket, and a carved floral or pinwheel design at the tip.

Of all the kitchen utensils produced by scrimshanders, in terms of sheer numbers and variety of design the pie crimper or jagging wheel is the winner, hands down. Designed to cut a rolled out pie crust (and also crimp together the top and bottom crusts of a pie), the crimper was another challenge for the scrimshander. The range of designs, from simple wheels with carved or turned handles to incredibly elaborate multi-wheel creations, is

49. A quartet of crimpers: top to bottom, *a turned example with red wax inlay, 5¼ in. (13.3 cm.); a five-point star wheel hub distinguishes this piece, 5⅞ in. (14.9 cm.); a crimper constructed of tortoiseshell over ivory, 6 in. (15.2 cm.); the serpent handle, a recurring design, 7 in. (17.8 cm.).*
Sources: Weston Howland, 83.452, 83.450, 83.399; Rodney W. Williams, 83.388

astounding. Though this collection is limited to single-wheel examples, there is no sense of sameness among the dozens of designs represented. The business end of the crimper is the cutting wheel, almost always meticulously carved and filed from whale ivory. An axle pin and carved yoke allow the wheel to turn. From there the scrimshander was free to pursue designs simple or complex. A few small examples feature a straight turned handle, sometimes with grooves inlaid with colored sealing wax [49].

The wheel hub of another whale-ivory example is carved in the shape of a five-point star [49]. Its open handle is clearly carved without aid of any mechanical tool. The hole at the tip of the handle is almost certainly for holding a hanging ring or cord.

Pie crimpers were not limited to ivory in their construction. Thin slabs of tortoiseshell are sandwiched over a whale-ivory core in another example [49]. A carved block of whale ivory at the tip balances the ivory wheel at the opposite end. Baleen too found its way into crimper construction. A serpent-handled specimen [49] incorporates a thin baleen segment in its shaft. While the serpent motif is thought by some to carry sexual meanings,[18] it nonetheless turns up in domestic articles like crimpers.

Some crimpers incorporate a two-, three- or four-tine fork as part of their overall design. The fork could be used in piercing steam vent holes in a pie crust before baking. Geometric shapes abound on such pieces, including

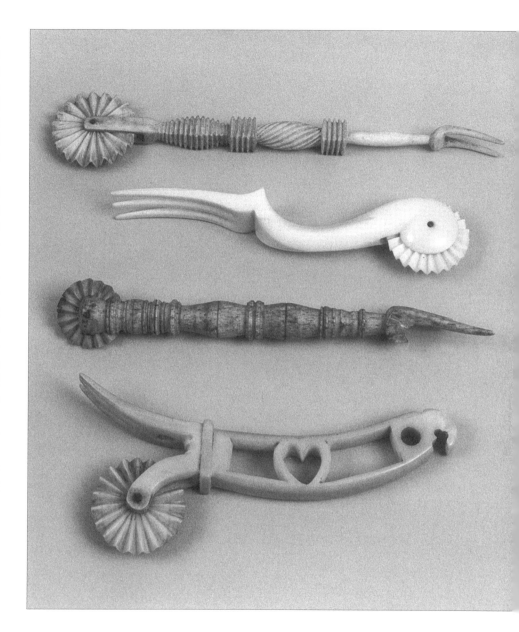

50. Some pie crimpers incorporated forks in their designs: top to bottom, *a masterpiece of filework, 8⅛ in. (20.6 cm.); a graceful curved handle ending in a fork, 6¼ in (15.9 cm.); an older, simpler design, 7¼ in. (18.4 cm.); the open heart bespeaks a whaleman's love, 6 in. (15.2 cm.).*
Sources: Weston Howland, 83.324, 83.322; Estate of John D. Hewlett, 89.3.25; Weston Howland, 83.525

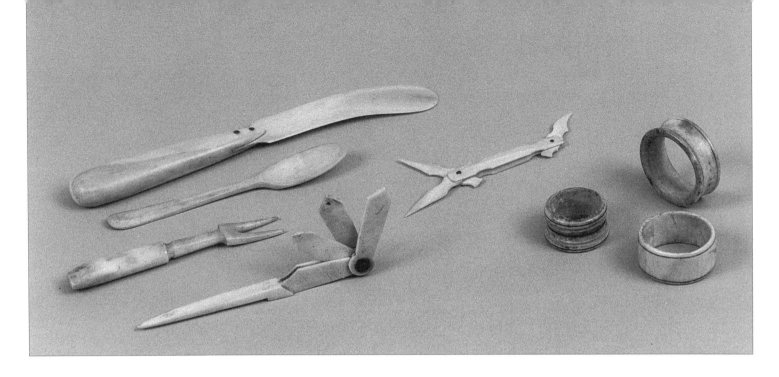

one multi-segmented whale-ivory example [50] in the collection. The maker of this heavily patinated crimper was a master with a file, creating even rope twist detailing. In striking contrast to the above is a crimper [50] whose whale-ivory wheel and graceful curved fork-handle have retained a creamy translucence.

Although ivory was the material of choice for pie crimpers, there are panbone examples as well. A long narrow specimen [50] with a small wheel is reminiscent of older crimpers in the simplicity of its construction. A clear reminder that crimpers were for the most part a labor of love for a wife or sweetheart can be found in an open-carved example [cover, 50] in the collection. While the open heart speaks volumes for the scrimshander's feelings, the parrot-like shape of the handle itself adds a bit of whimsy to the final product.

51. From soup to nuts, miscellaneous dining utensils include ivory butter knife, 7½ in. (19 cm.); panbone spoon, 4¾ in. (12.1 cm.); and small ivory fork, 4 in. (10.2 cm.). Among folding whale ivory toothpicks are one, bottom, with broad blades, 4⅜ in. (11.1 cm.); and a smaller example, top, attributed to a Long Island whaleman, 3¼ in. (8.3 cm.). Turned ivory napkin rings range in diameter from 1⅛ (2.8 cm.) to 1½ in. (3.9 cm.).
Sources: Weston Howland, 83.227, 83.379.2; Anonymous, 83.380.1; Weston Howland, 83.403; Museum Purchase, 91.12.3; Weston Howland, 83.239, 83.447.4, 83.459.3

Dining utensils were also within the scrimshander's realm of activity, though the beauty and variety of the objects he created frequently stood in stark contrast to those in use in the fo'c'sle. Knives, forks, spoons, and related items were produced [51] in some quantity. While it is unlikely that anything as refined as napkin rings were used by foremast hands, the officers might very well dine with such amenities. Consider the comment of Wilson Andrews of the New Bedford whaleship *Hibernia*: "Carpenter turning Napkin Rings for Old Man & Mate. So ends this day."[19] Napkin rings in the collection [51] include examples made from whale and walrus ivory, some with red and blue wax inlays.

While not strictly dining utensils, toothpicks were also a functional product from the hands of scrimshanders. One example [51] measuring nearly 4½ inches in length features three folding blades and is marked with the initials "W S" or "S M." Of note is another whale-ivory example [51] with scimitar-like blades at both ends. It descended in the Foster family of East Hampton and was probably made by one of three brothers – Alfred, Philetus, or Elijah Foster – who served in the Long Island whaling fleet in the 1840s.[20]

Odds and Ends

Most collections contain miscellaneous household items that do not fit comfortably into such categories as clothing accessories or kitchen utensils. A number are worthy of note, either in representing groups of similar items in the collection, or for being unusual in some way.

Some household utensils are mundane by nature; yet at the hands of a scrimshaw craftsman these functional pieces can take on a marvelous grace in their simplicity.

52. Functional forms – panbone clothespins: **left to right, turned with wax inlay, 4¾ in. (12.1 cm.); an example with a faceted cube head, 4⅞ in. (12.5 cm.); a bulbous head type, 5 in. (12.7 cm.); a simple turned specimen, 5⅛ in. (13 cm.).** *Sources:* Weston Howland, 83.272.4,8,6; Anonymous, 83.271.1

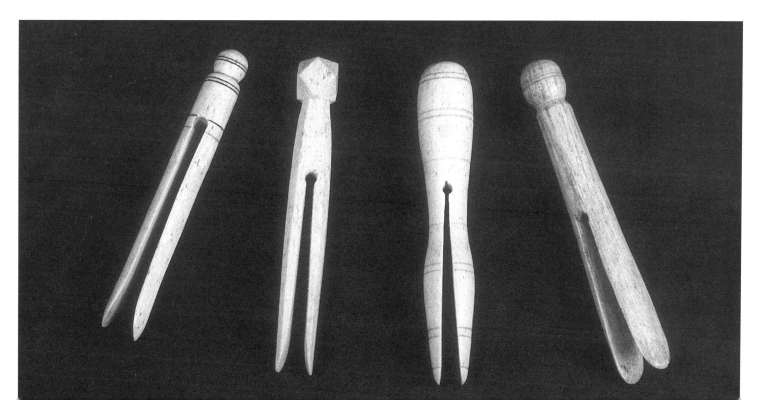

For example, a clothespin is a clothespin is a clothespin; yet a selection of panbone examples from the collection [52] exhibits a wide range of decorative treatments and effects. Turned and scribed, three of the four clothespins illustrated suggest that some importance was given to their design and appearance. The fourth example, with polyhedron knob and beveled sides, is the product of much labor with file and saw.

Until the development of oil lamps with self-raising burner wicks, the task of raising and adjusting a wick fell to the wick pick. Basically this was a fine stylus or needle point with a handle of some kind. Whalemen used their skill in filing and turning to produce marvelous examples in ivory and panbone. A whale-ivory example [53] in the collection typifies the design – a heavy and stable base into

Above, 53. A handy lamp accessory – a wick pick, 5¾ in. (14.6 cm.).
Source: Anonymous, 83.242

which the pick is placed when not in use, and an elaborately turned handle.

A general purpose storage container [54] bears unmistakable proof of the loving intent of its maker. Riveted copper bands provide support for the heavy panbone staves that form the sides of this eleven-inch-long elliptical tub. Though not waterproof, the tub could hold sewing or general household items. The quality of the tub's construction suggests that perhaps it was the work of a ship's cooper.

Left, 54. An unusual storage container – a miniature panbone tub, 11 x 8¾ in. (27.9 x 22.2 cm.).
Source: Weston Howland, 83.580

Occasionally toys and models of various kinds were made by whalemen. While some articles were clearly made for use by children, the intent of others is less clear. A good example of the latter is a splendid model believed to be St. John's Episcopal Church [55] in Cold Spring Harbor. Sitting at the head of the harbor since 1836, the same year the Cold Spring Whaling Company was organized, St. John's Church [56] long served as a landmark to local navigators.[21] As modeled by an unidentified scrimshander the church has been slightly reduced in size. Careful workmanship has reproduced shingle and siding details that add much to the overall effect. The whale-ivory structure is placed upon a rectangular wood base with a rounded front.

55. A model of St. John's Church is a scrimshaw masterpiece, 5¾ x 3½ in. (14.6 x 8.9 cm.).
Source: Anonymous, 83.311

56. St. John's Church in Cold Spring Harbor, circa 1910.
Courtesy of the Huntington Historical Society

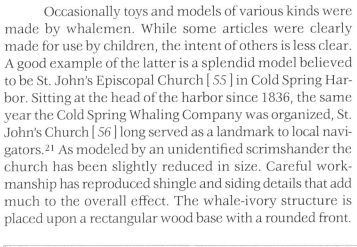

Cold Spring Har, N.Y.

• 55 •

57. Whaling logs frequently include stamps indicating whales taken or lost. This whale ivory example features a sperm whale, 1½ in. (3.8 cm.).
Source: Rodney W. Williams, 83.270

The base is overlayed with panbone with criss-cross incising, and the path to the front door is fashioned of baleen. Of added interest is the mother-of-pearl inlay in the path, crafted in a diamond-and-leaf pattern. Other details include tortoiseshell windows and a whale-ivory fence that surrounds the building and churchyard. This model is a singular example of the whaleman's art.

Tools of the Trade

Those who have never handled fresh panbone and ivory cannot conceive of the resiliency of such materials. Whalemen knew and appreciated the ruggedness of these raw materials and used them to good effect in producing tools that were as functional as they were handsome.

Stamps carved in the shape of whales were used by ships' log-keepers to note the capture of a whale. Carved from wood, ivory, panbone, or a combination of these materials, such whale stamps served a clear purpose on shipboard. There are several small examples in the collection [57] as well as a set of four wooden whale stamps carved by Robert Cushman Murphy during his 1912–13 voyage aboard the brig *Daisy*.

Rigging gear and tools [58] were also fabricated for use on shipboard. Pointed fids for splicing lines, plus blocks, thimbles, grommets, and other rigging items were crafted from fresh panbone and ivory. Seam rubbers [59], used by sailmakers to insure a sharp crease before stitching two pieces of canvas, were also frequently made of durable panbone. The natural self-lubricating qualities of fresh panbone, in fact, made it a logical material for seam rubbers, fids, and similar items.

The cooper, carpenter, or other ship's officers might fabricate tools for their own use. William Wilson, a crewman aboard the bark *Cavalier* of Stonington, Connecticut, noted in his journal that George Thompson, the vessel's African-American first mate, was busy "scrimshonting tools."[22] A number of such tools [60] can be found in the collection, among them a bow saw, marking gauge, mallet, and plane constructed in whole or in part of panbone. One of several rulers in the collection, which are made of wood and panbone or ivory, is also illustrated. Though now somewhat warped and brittle, when new such tools were perfectly serviceable, and stand as testaments to the craftsmanship of many a whaleman.

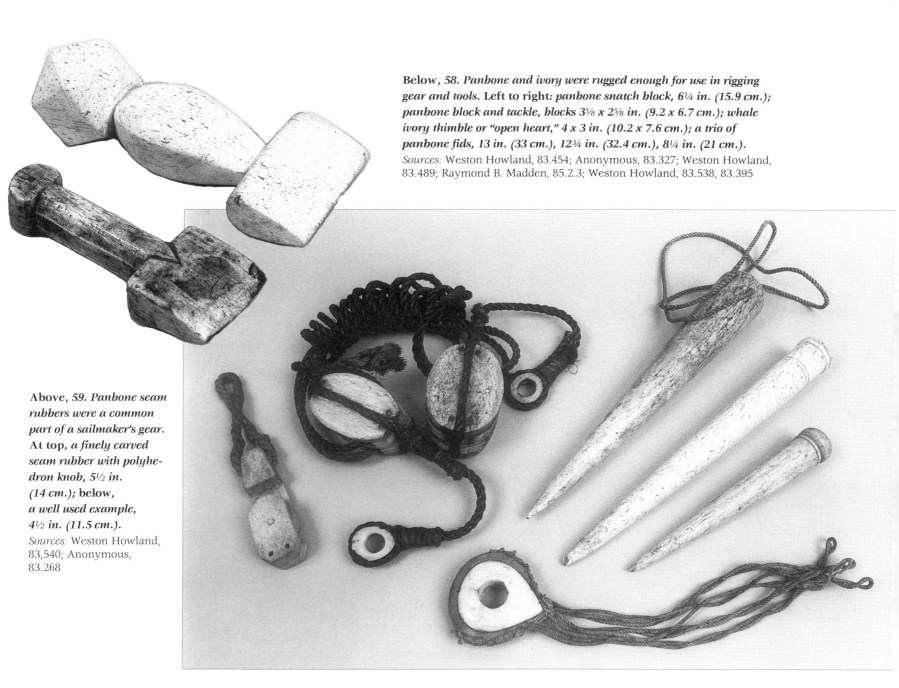

Below, 58. Panbone and ivory were rugged enough for use in rigging gear and tools. **Left to right:** *panbone snatch block, 6¼ in. (15.9 cm.); panbone block and tackle, blocks 3⅝ x 2⅝ in. (9.2 x 6.7 cm.); whale ivory thimble or "open heart," 4 x 3 in. (10.2 x 7.6 cm.); a trio of panbone fids, 13 in. (33 cm.), 12¾ in. (32.4 cm.), 8¼ in. (21 cm.).*
Sources: Weston Howland, 83.454; Anonymous, 83.327; Weston Howland, 83.489; Raymond B. Madden, 85.2.3; Weston Howland, 83.538, 83.395

Above, 59. Panbone seam rubbers were a common part of a sailmaker's gear. At top, *a finely carved seam rubber with polyhedron knob, 5½ in. (14 cm.);* **below,** *a well used example, 4½ in. (11.5 cm.).*
Sources: Weston Howland, 83,540; Anonymous, 83.268

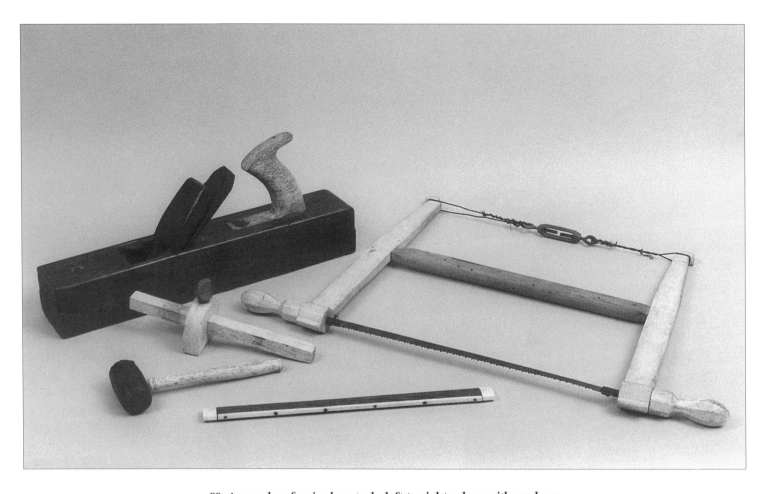

60. A sampler of scrimshaw tools, left to right: *plane with panbone handle, 16 in. (40.6 cm.); panbone marking gauge, 8⅞ in. (22.6 cm.); lignum vitae mallet with panbone handle, 7¼ in. (18.4 cm.); walrus ivory and wood ruler, 12½ in. (31.8 cm.); panbone and wood bow saw, 23¼ x 14¾ in. (59.1 x 37.5 cm.).*
Sources: Weston Howland, 83.197, 83.456, 83.269, 83.223; Anonymous, 83.410

Reconsidering the "Penney" Tooth

*My lay to take charge of the Bark Alice of Cold
Spring will be the 13th lay and a bonus of 500
hundred dollars cash; to be paid when I ship . . .*

George G Penny.[1]

The cataloging of any collection of scrimshaw is sure to raise questions about individual examples for which there are no easy or satisfactory answers. This project has been no different in this respect.

The amount of scholarly research in the field of scrimshaw has grown tremendously in the past twenty-five years. Building on the earlier work of people like Everett U. Crosby, Maurius Barbeau, and Edward Daland, to name a few, contemporary researchers have undertaken more systematic studies of the materials, techniques, and iconography associated with this folk art form. The increase in the number of scrimshaw fakes and forgeries, whether crafted in the scrimshander's traditional materials or modern polymer-based substances, underscores the need for such new approaches. Some decry this trend as being overly analytical at the expense of what has been called the "romance" of scrimshaw. Yet, in learning more about the "how" and "what" of this art form we have gained an even greater appreciation of the artistic and craft achievements of the whaleman.

The increase in the market value of scrimshaw in recent decades has spurred much of the interest in systematic analysis. The probability of intentional forgeries has raised the stakes in this field as it long has in the art market as a whole. Now private collectors and institutions alike take a harder look at prospective scrimshaw acquisitions.

At the same time, cataloging projects like that upon which this monograph is based provide an opportunity to reexamine items whose authenticity has never been questioned. It is not a process without risks, to be sure; but it is a process that should be undertaken in striving for a more accurate understanding of this marvelous art. While questions have now been raised about the age and authenticity of at least a score of pieces in the collection, it is the case of the "Penney" tooth that best illustrates both the need for such reexamination and some of the techniques now being employed.

Since its acquisition in 1956 as part of the Weston Howland collection, the Penney tooth [*61*] has been one of the best known pieces in the museum's collection.

Bearing the name of a Long Island whaleman who eventually commanded a Cold Spring Harbor whaler, and including a marvelous portrait of a Long Island whaling vessel, this tooth has long been considered among the most important examples in the collection.

George G. Penny (1816–88), a native of Shelter Island, sailed aboard vessels from several ports, including the *Washington* of Greenport during its 1848–51 voyage. In an 1854 letter to Cold Spring Harbor whaling agent John

H. Jones, Penny mentioned that he had last served aboard the Stonington, Connecticut, whaleship *Betsey Williams*.[2] A check of Starbuck's *History of the American Whale Fishery* indicates that this would have been the ship's final voyage from Stonington, 1851–54, before its sale to New Bedford.[3] Penny's negotiations with Jones bore fruit, and

62. **Note the initials "G P" on the reverse of the "Penney" tooth, 6⅝ in. (16.8 cm.).**
Source: Weston Howland, 83.301

from October 1854 to May 1858 he was master of the bark *Alice* of Cold Spring Harbor. By all accounts this was his sole command, and his subsequent career remains a mystery. The tooth strongly implies service aboard the *Concordia* of Sag Harbor, but no date is given. If Penny indeed served aboard the *Concordia* it must have been after his command of the *Alice*, as he made no mention of the Sag Harbor vessel in his letter to Jones.

In an art form characterized by anonymous practitioners a boldly engraved signature draws great interest. And yet this element poses some questions. The surname Penney can also be spelled "Penny" and, based on a review of genealogical records from Shelter Island as well as signed letters in the museum's archival collection, he used the latter spelling.[4] This alone, however, is not sufficient basis to question the authenticity of the piece, for even Starbuck's *History of the American Whale Fishery* and the 1850 census recorded the "Penney" spelling. The novel spelling of the given name as "Gorge" seemed unusual; and the same whaling documents mentioned above clearly show that he spelled his name "George." It seems unlikely that he would deliberately misspell his name on such a piece; or that, if engraved as a gift from a friend or colleague, it would be so spelled.

As noted, the fact of Penny's service aboard the *Concordia* has been based to date on the tooth alone. While it is certainly possible that Penny sailed aboard the vessel during one of her four voyages from Sag Harbor in the years following his command of the *Alice*, it is the engraved portrait of the *Concordia* that raises the greatest doubt about the tooth. Whalemen were certainly not trained artists, and a good deal of their work, excepting that slavishly copied from printed illustrations, reflects this fact. Nevertheless, while they might not have a good grasp of such artistic skills as the use of perspective, they were generally quite accurate in depicting their vessels and activities. The *Concordia* was rigged as a bark throughout her long whaling career, 1837–71. Yet, the tooth clearly shows a ship rig. It is simply inconceivable that George Penny or any other whaleman would make such a blatant error.

The opposite side of the tooth [62] bears a wonderful vignette portraying a young couple holding hands, the whole being surrounded by a vine-work border with green-inked leaves. The style of clothing suggests the 1830s or perhaps 1840s; and in fact there is nothing to suggest that this work does not date to that period. The initials "G P" engraved at the lower right corner will be discussed shortly. A nice patina is evident on this side of the tooth.

In comparing the two sides it is evident that two different hands were involved. The side bearing the signature and vessel portrait is much more carefully planned, deeply incised, and boldly inked than the opposite face. There is also noticeably less patination on this side.

In recent years a good deal of research has been done on the surface characteristics of scrimshaw teeth. Pioneering efforts in this line have been made by Desmond Liddy in Australia, and his findings have been shared with collectors and scholars in this country at various symposia.[5] With the aid of a 30X stereo microscope surface details can be examined and, more importantly, compared with those of documented period teeth.

Surface preparation seems to be consistent on both sides, with many small scratch marks running parallel to the grain. Such marks are characteristic of period work. The check or crack running across the vignette side shows the dirt and dust accumulation usually associated with an old tooth. As mentioned, however, the degree of patination between the sides is different, with the vessel side having less. In addition, tiny paint droplets that are frequently found on old teeth (an indication, according to Liddy, of the low value placed on them in the past) are more numerous on the vignette side than the vessel side. The suggestion here is that, while both sides were prepared for engraving at the same time, the vessel side was engraved at a later date than the vignette side, and received a surface cleaning before the new work was commenced. An alternate explanation is that, since only the vignette side was originally engraved, this side was more likely to be exposed to the long term effects of light and handling.

Supporting the idea that the vessel side was engraved at a later date and by a different hand is the fact that the initials "G P" on the vignette side are engraved right across the boldest part of the leaf border design. It seems unlikely that the engraver of the vignette would have done this. In addition, when these initials were inked (in black) the ink flowed beyond the initials into the intersecting areas of the leaf, covering portions of the green ink.

Thus we are left with serious questions about this tooth, not the least of which are: "Who were the engravers?"; "When was each side engraved?"; and "What was the intent in engraving the vessel side of the tooth?" Unfortunately, the source from which Weston Howland acquired this tooth was not recorded,[6] so we can only speculate on many of these questions.

In time, more clues may be uncovered that will shed some light on the "Penney tooth." However, based on the available data and an analysis of the physical evidence, the attribution of this piece to George Penny must remain questionable at best. Somehow it seems fitting that, in a folk art so intimately connected with the sea, beguiling mysteries like this should remain to kindle our sense of inquiry and wonder.

APPENDIX I

Scrimshanders Represented in the Collection

Bongo, Peter (contemporary)
    83.343; tooth
Enos, Manuel, attributed to
    83.300.1–2; teeth
    89.3.1AB; walrus tusks
Foster, Alfred, Elijah, or Philetus, attributed to
    91.12.3; toothpick
Hanes (?), A. H.
    83.549; busk
J., B. T.
    83.483; tooth
King, C.
    83.4; cane
L., A.
    83.543; seam rubber
Mitchell, Samuel, attributed to
    83.544.1–2; cufflinks
Murphy, Robert Cushman
    83.534.1–4; whale stamps
P., C. M., attributed to
    83.531; busk
S., H.
    83.197; plane
S., H. F., attributed to
    83.325; pie crimper

S., P. N.
    83.366; tooth
Sherman, Jesse T., attributed to
    83.377; brooch
Williams, Joseph
    83.470; busk

APPENDIX II

Vessels, People and Places
Represented in the Collection

Vessels

Essex, American whaleship
    83.343; tooth (modern work)
Java, American whaling bark
    89.3.1A; walrus tusk
O. M. Remington, American whaling schooner
    83.364; tooth

People and Places

Betsy (?)
    83.257; toothpick
Boston, Massachusetts
    83.514; tooth
Cincinnati, Ohio
    83.483; tooth
Clark, Mary
    83.215; busk
Fisher's Island, New York
    90.5; baleen
Hawaiian Islands (?)
    83.362; tooth
Justice, figure of
    83.373; tooth
Long Island, New York
    90.5; baleen
Long Island Sound
    90.5; baleen
Minot's Ledge Lighthouse
    83.514; tooth
New Bedford, Massachusetts
    83.470; busk
Sally (?)
    83.257; toothpick
Washington, George
    83.523; tooth

NOTES

Notes to Chapter 1

1. "Logbook of the Brig *Orion*, Obed Luce Master," 14 March 1821, Log 293, G. W. Blunt White Library, Mystic Seaport Museum.

2. For a more complete discussion of the various theories see chapter 1 of either E. Norman Flayderman, *Scrimshaw and Scrimshanders* (New Milford, Conn.: N. Flayderman & Co., 1972) or Richard C. Malley, *Graven by the fishermen themselves: Scrimshaw in Mystic Seaport Museum* (Mystic: Mystic Seaport Museum, 1983).

3. Dr. Janet West of the Scott Polar Research Institute at Cambridge University in England has undertaken the first systematic study of Australian scrimshaw.

4. Richard C. Malley, "On Shore in a Foreign Land: Mary Stark in the Kingdom of Hawaii," *The Log of Mystic Seaport* 37, 3 (Fall 1985): 79–92; and Malley, *Graven by the fishermen themselves*, pp. 88–90.

5. Richard W. Updike, "The walrus and the commodore – a puzzle in scrimshaw," *Antiques* 98, 2 (August 1970): 263–65.

6. Stuart M. Frank's *Dictionary of Scrimshaw Artists* (Mystic: Mystic Seaport Museum, 1991) is a pioneering effort in the study of identified scrimshanders.

7. Joshua Basseches and Stuart M. Frank's study, *Edward Burdett, 1805–1833: America's First Master Scrimshaw Artist* (Sharon, Massachusetts: Kendall Whaling Museum, 1991), is a good example of such recent scholarship.

8. Journal of Edwin P. Brown aboard bark *Noble*, 28 September 1841. Quoted in *In the Wake of Whales: The Whaling Journals of Capt. Edwin Peter Brown, 1841–1847* (Orient, New York: Old Orient Press, 1988).

9. "Journal of a whaling voyage kept on board the Ship *New England* of New London by Henry Rogers," 6 September 1859, Connecticut Historical Society, Hartford, Connecticut.

10. Journal of Lucy Hix Crapo aboard the bark *Louisa* of New Bedford, 6 August 1866, Log 899, G. W. Blunt White Library, Mystic Seaport Museum.

11. "Journal of Gurdon Hall aboard the Ship *Charles Phelps*," 29 February 1844, Log 141, G. W. Blunt White Library, Mystic Seaport Museum.

12. A letter from New York merchants Colvill & Fleming to New London merchant J. N. Harris, 24 April 1842, inquires about the availability of large sperm whale teeth for commercial uses, Misc. Letters, Connecticut Historical Society; Frederick A. Olmstead also mentions some commercial value for sperm whale teeth in his *Incidents of a Whaling Voyage* (New York: D. Appleton and Co., 1841), p. 181.

13. Augusta Penniman, "Remarks made on board Bark *Minerva*, during a whale voyage to the Arctic Ocean," 8 August 1867, quoted in *Journal of a Whaling Voyage* (Eastham, Massachusetts: Eastern National Park and Monument Association, 1988).

14. "Journal of a whaling voyage kept on board the Ship *New England* of New London by Henry Rogers," 2 July 1859, Connecticut Historical Society.

15. "Journal of Gurdon Hall aboard the Ship *Charles Phelps*," 26 January 1844, Log 141, G. W. Blunt White Library, Mystic Seaport Museum.

16. Joseph F. Caron, "Scrimshaw and Its Importance as an American Folk Art" (Ph.D. diss., Illinois State University, 1977), p. 74.

Notes to Chapter 2

1. *Paumanok* was the Native-American name for Long Island.

2. Marilyn Weigold, *The American Mediterranean: An Environmental, Economic & Social History of Long Island Sound* (Port Washington, New York: Kennikat Press, 1974), p. 126.

3. John H. Jones, *The Jones Family of Long Island* (New York: Tobias A. Wright, 1907), p. 79.

4. Weigold, *American Mediterranean*, p. 36.

5. Augustus Griffin, *Griffin's Journal* (Orient, New York: Oysterponds Historical Society, 1983), p. 70.

6. Harriet G. and Andrus T. Valentine, *An Island People: One Foot in the Sea, One on Shore* (Huntington, New York: authors, 1976), pp. 59–61.

7. Geoffrey L. Rossano, "Prosperity on the Ways: Shipbuilding in Colonial Oyster Bay, 1745–1775," *The Long Island Historical Journal* 2 (Fall 1989): 27.

8. Harriet G. Valentine, *The Window on the Street* (Smithtown, New York: Exposition Press, 1981), p. 72. Helen Rogers's diary mentions considerable trade to the Caribbean and Gulf from Cold Spring Harbor.

9. Admiral Harold E. Shear, "My Life in Bunker Boats," paper presented at the Tenth Annual Symposium on Southern New England Maritime History, Mystic Seaport Museum, 3 November 1990.

10. Lawrence J. Taylor, "Oystering on Long Island in Comparative Perspective," *The Long Island Historical Journal* 2 (Fall 1989): 64–68.

11. John Strong, "Shinnecock and Montauk Whalemen," *The Long Island Historical Journal* 2 (Fall 1989): 29.

12. K. Jack Bauer, *A Maritime History of the United States* (Columbia: University of South Carolina Press, 1988), p. 230.

13. William R. Palmer, "The Whaling Port of Sag Harbor" (Ph.D. diss., Columbia University, 1964), pp. 13–14.

14. Alexander Starbuck, *History of the American Whale Fishery*, 2 vols., (1878; reprint, New York: Argosy-Antiquarian, Ltd., 1964), p. 43.

15. John Gardner, "Whaleboat Warfare on the Sound," *The Log of Mystic Seaport* 28, 2 (July 1976): 59–60.

16. Frederick P. Schmidt, *Mark Well the Whale,* 2nd ed., (Cold Spring Harbor, New York: Whaling Museum Society, Inc., 1986), pp. 138–39. Schmidt's study is the best on the whaling industry of Cold Spring Harbor.

17. Benjamin F. Thompson, *History of Long Island*, 2 vols., 3rd ed., (New York: Robert H. Dodd, 1918), 2:187. Starbuck does not list any Jamesport vessels, but does list returns of one vessel being landed at the village during each of the years 1839–42. It is possible that this vessel sailed from Sag Harbor or Greenport but was owned in Jamesport.

18. Robert Lloyd Webb, *On the Northwest: Commercial Whaling in the Pacific Northwest, 1790–1967* (Vancouver: University of British Columbia Press, 1988), p. 50.

19. Thomas Welcome Roys gave the honor for taking the first bowhead whale to the Cold Spring Harbor whaleship *Huntsville* in 1848. Evidence suggests that a Danish whaleship, *Neptun*, had taken bowheads in 1845. See Frederick P. Schmidt, *et al, Thomas Welcome Roys* (Charlottesville: University Press of Virginia, 1980), p. 26; and Webb, *On the Northwest*, p. 317, note 168.

20. Data compiled from various sources including Starbuck's *History of the American Whale Fishery*, Schmidt's *Mark Well the Whale!*, and Finckenor's *Whales and Whaling: Port of Sag Harbor*.

21. Palmer, "The Whaling Port of Sag Harbor," p. 292.

22. Floris Barnet Cash, "African-American Whalers: Images and Reality," *Long Island Historical Journal* 2 (Fall 1989): 41–43.

23. Robert Cushman Murphy, "The Pre-History and Beginnings of the Whaling Museum," paper presented at the Whaling Museum, Cold Spring Harbor, New York, 15 September, 1967, published as *The Founding of the Whaling Museum at Cold Spring Harbor, L.I., N.Y.* (Cold Spring Harbor, New York: Whaling Museum Society, 1967).

24. Author's correspondence with Weston Howland, Jr., 20 June 1991.

Notes to Chapter 3

1. Journal of Wilson Andrews aboard the ship *Hibernia*, 16 April 1869, Log 81, G. W. Blunt White Library, Mystic Seaport Museum.

2. "Journal of a whaling voyage kept on board the Ship *New England* of New London by Henry Rogers," 8 May 1858, Connecticut Historical Society, Hartford, Connecticut.

3. Journal kept aboard the bark *Alice*, 4 September 1859, Cold Spring Harbor Whaling Museum.

4. Author's correspondence with Robert L. Webb, 28 May 1991.

5. Robert L. Webb, "'Old Moke' Afloat: Notes on the Minstrel Origins of the Banjo at Sea," *The Log of Mystic Seaport* 35, 4 (Winter 1984): 110–11.

6. "Journal of Gurdon Hall aboard the Ship *Charles Phelps*," 12 November 1842, Log 141, G. W. Blunt White Library, Mystic Seaport Museum.

7. Journal of Francis Cook aboard the ship *Sheffield*, 26 December 1845, Cold Spring Harbor Whaling Museum.

8. Clifford W. Ashley, *The Yankee Whaler* (Boston: Houghton Mifflin, 1926), p. 114.

9. Journal of Francis Cook aboard the ship *Sheffield*, 18 May 1846, Cold Spring Harbor Whaling Museum.

10. There is considerable confusion about Enos's whaling career in Cold Spring Harbor vessels, though his service aboard the bark *Java* is well documented. In an article in *Long Island Forum* (March 1954), local historian Andrus T. Valentine relates Enos's return home to Cold Spring Harbor with these tusks, but he does not cite his source of information.

11. Journal kept aboard the bark *Alice*, 30 April 1860, Cold Spring Harbor Whaling Museum.

12. Journal of Edwin P. Brown aboard the ship *Lucy Ann*, 24 September 1846, quoted in *In the Wake of Whales: The Whaling Journals of Capt. Edwin Peter Brown, 1841–1847* (Orient, New York: Old Orient Press, 1988).

13. Journal of Francis Cook aboard the ship *Sheffield*, 11 November 1845, Cold Spring Harbor Whaling Museum.

14. Margaret L. Vose, "Selected Design Sources for Scrimshaw, a Folk Art of the New England Whaling Industry, 1775–1900" (Ph.D. diss., New York University, 1992), pp. 214ff."

Notes to Chapter 4

1. "Journal of Gurdon Hall aboard the Ship *Charles Phelps*," 30 January 1844, Log 141, G. W. Blunt White Library, Mystic Seaport Museum.

2. Ibid., 16 February 1844.

3. Margaret L. Vose, "Selected Design Sources for Scrimshaw, a Folk Art of the New England Whaling Industry, 1775–1900" (Ph.D. diss., New York University, 1992), pp. 201ff.

4. Ibid., 162ff.

5. Author's correspondence with Paul Cyr, New Bedford Free Public Library, 19 October 1990.

6. Quoted in Arthur C. Watson, *The Long Harpoon* (New Bedford: George H. Reynolds, 1929), p. 162.

7. Journal of Wilson Andrews aboard the ship *Hibernia*, 8 January 1869, Log 81, G. W. Blunt White Library, Mystic Seaport Museum.

8. "Journal of a whaling voyage kept on board the Ship *New England* of New London by Henry Rogers," 3 November 1858, Connecticut Historical Society, Hartford, Connecticut.

9. "Journal of Gurdon Hall aboard the Ship *Charles Phelps*," 19 February 1844, Log 141, G.W. Blunt White Library, Mystic Seaport Museum.

10. *Ship Registers and Enrollments of New Bedford, Mass., 1796–1939* (Boston: The National Archives Project, 1940), pp. 19, 115, 124; and logbook of the bark *Thomas Dickason*, New Bedford Whaling Museum.

11. Whaling Museum Society, *Annual Report*, 1953; and miscellaneous manuscript items, Cold Spring Harbor Whaling Museum.

12. Charles Manghis, "Swifts," paper presented at Scrimshaw Collectors' Weekend, Kendall Whaling Museum, 25 April 1992.

13. According to Dr. Margaret L. Vose, such knitting sheaths were widely used in Britain. See also Richard Rutt, *A History of Hand Knitting* (Loveland, Colorado: Interweave Press, 1987), pp. 20, 125.

14. Vose, "Selected Design Sources for Scrimshaw," pp. 189ff.

15. For more information on the origins and variations of the fylfot, see Vose, "Selected Design Sources for Scrimshaw," pp. 136ff.

16. "Journal of Gurdon Hall aboard the Ship *Charles Phelps*," 8 February 1844, Log 141, G. W. Blunt White Library, Mystic Seaport Museum.

17. Journal of Frederick Crapser aboard the bark *Pantheon*, 24 February 1844, Log 769, G. W. Blunt White Library, Mystic Seaport Museum.

18. E. Norman Flayderman, *Scrimshaw and Scrimshanders* (New Milford, Connecticut: N. Flayderman & Co., 1972), pp. 184, 189.

19. Journal of Wilson Andrews aboard the ship *Hibernia*, 30 September 1868, Log 81, G. W. Blunt White Library, Mystic Seaport Museum.

20. A large collection of Foster family material, including whaling journals kept by the brothers, was sold at an East Hampton auction in 1991.

21. St. John's Church, *The Parish Register: Part II, Special 150th Anniversary Edition* (Cold Spring Harbor, New York: St. John's Church, 1985), pp. 3–5.

22. Journal of William H. Wilson aboard the bark *Cavalier*, 7 December 1849, Log 18, G. W. Blunt White Library, Mystic Seaport Museum.

Notes to Chapter 5

1. George G. Penny to John H. Jones, 10 August 1854, Cold Spring Harbor Whaling Museum.

2. Ibid.

3. Penny mentioned the voyage's length as about thirty-three months which, according to Starbuck's *History of the American Whale Fishery,* perfectly matches the 1851–54 voyage of the ship *Betsey Williams.*

4. According to genealogical records at the Shelter Island Historical Society, "Penny" is the more common spelling of this surname locally.

5. The Kendall Whaling Museum has sponsored scrimshaw symposia annually since 1989. The information included here was presented by Desmond Liddy in several papers at the 1991 and 1992 meetings.

6. Author's correspondence with Weston Howland, Jr., 23 August 1991.

BIBLIOGRAPHY

"*Alice*, Logbook of the Bark, 1854–1858." Cold Spring Harbor Whaling Museum, Cold Spring Harbor, New York.

"*Alice*, Journal Kept Aboard the Bark, 1858–1860." Cold Spring Harbor Whaling Museum, Cold Spring Harbor, New York.

Andrews, Wilson. "Journal of a Whaling Voyage Aboard the Ship *Hibernia,* 1866–1869." G. W. Blunt White Library, Mystic Seaport Museum, Mystic, Connecticut.

Ashley, Clifford W. *The Yankee Whaler.* Boston: Houghton Mifflin Co., 1926.

Barbeau, Maurius. "All Hands Aboard Scrimshawing." *American Neptune* 12 (1952): 99–122.

_____. "Seafaring Folk Art." *Antiques* 66 (1954): 47–49.

Basseches, Joshua, and Stuart M. Frank. *Edward Burdett, 1805–1833: America's First Master Scrimshaw Artist.* Kendall Whaling Museum Monograph Series, No. 5. Sharon, Massachusetts: Kendall Whaling Museum, 1991.

Bauer, K. Jack. *A Maritime History of the United States.* Columbia: University of South Carolina Press, 1988.

Brown, Edwin Peter. *In the Wake of Whales: The Whaling Journals of Capt. Edwin Peter Brown, 1841–1847.* Orient, New York: Old Orient Press, 1988.

Caron, Joseph F. "Scrimshaw and Its Importance as an American Folk Art." Ph.D. diss., Illinois State University, 1976. Ann Arbor: University Microfilms International, 1977.

Carpenter, Charles H., Jr. "Early Dated Scrimshaw." *Antiques* 102 (1972): 414–19.

Cash, Floris Barnet. "African-American Whalers: Images and Reality." *The Long Island Historical Journal* 2 (1989): 41–52.

Colvill & Fleming. Letter to J. N. Harris, 24 April 1842. Connecticut Historical Society, Hartford, Connecticut.

Cook, Francis. "Journal of a Voyage Aboard the Ship *Sheffield*, 1845–1847." Cold Spring Harbor Whaling Museum, Cold Spring Harbor, New York.

Crapo, Lucy Hix. "Journal of a Whaling Voyage Aboard the Bark *Louisa*, 1866–1867." G. W. Blunt White Library, Mystic Seaport Museum, Mystic, Connecticut.

Cropser, Frederick. "Journal of a Whaling Voyage Aboard the Bark *Pantheon*, 1842–1845." G. W. Blunt White Library, Mystic Seaport Museum, Mystic, Connecticut.

Crosby, Everett U. *Susan's Teeth and Much Ado about Scrimshaw.* Nantucket, Massachusetts: Everett U. Crosby, 1955.

Daland, Edward L. "Engraved Types of Scrimshaw." *Antiques* 28 (1935): 153–55.

Decker, Robert Owen. *The Whaling City: A History of New London.* Chester, Connecticut: Pequot Press, 1976.

Dunbaugh, Edwin L. "The Montauk Steamboat Company." *The Long Island Historical Journal* 2 (1989): 52–63.

Earle, Walter K. *Out of the Wilderness.* Cold Spring Harbor, New York: Whaling Museum Society, 1966.

_____. *Scrimshaw: Folk Art of the Whalers.* Cold Spring Harbor, New York: Whaling Museum Society, 1957.

Farwell, Robert D. "Manuel Enos: Cold Spring Whaleman." *Long Island Forum* (June 1981): 108–09.

Finckenor, George A. *Whales and Whaling: Port of Sag Harbor, New York.* Sag Harbor, New York: William Ewers, 1975.

Flayderman, E. Norman. *Scrimshaw and Scrimshanders: Whales and Whalemen*. New Milford, Connecticut: N. Flayderman & Co., 1972.

Frank, Stuart M. *Biographical Dictionary of Scrimshaw Artists in the Kendall Whaling Museum*. Kendall Whaling Museum Monograph Series, No. 4. Sharon, Massachusetts: Kendall Whaling Museum, 1989.

_____. *Dictionary of Scrimshaw Artists*. Mystic, Connecticut: Mystic Seaport Museum, 1991.

_____. *Fakeshaw: A Checklist of Plastic "Scrimshaw."* Kendall Whaling Museum Monograph Series, No. 1. Sharon, Massachusetts: Kendall Whaling Museum, 1988.

Gabriel, Ralph Henry. *The Evolution of Long Island: A Story of Land and Sea*. 1921. Reprint. Port Washington, New York: Ira J. Friedman, Inc., 1960.

Gardner, John. "Whaleboat Warfare on the Sound." *The Log of Mystic Seaport* 28 (1976): 59–68.

German, Andrew W. "Connecticut's Changing Relationship with Long Island Sound." *The Long Island Historical Journal* 2 (1989): 76–89.

Gilkerson, William. *The Scrimshander*. Rev. ed. San Francisco: Troubador Press, 1978.

Goldenberg, Joseph A. *Shipbuilding in Colonial America*. Charlottesville: University Press of Virginia, 1976.

Goode, G. Brown, ed. *The Fisheries and Fishery Industries of the United States*. Washington, D.C.: Government Printing Office, 1884–87.

Griffin, Augustus. *Griffin's Journal*. 1857. Reprint. Orient, New York: Oysterponds Historical Society, 1983.

Hall, Gurdon. "Journal of a Voyage aboard the Ship *Charles Phelps*, 1842–1844." G. W. Blunt White Library, Mystic Seaport Museum, Mystic, Connecticut.

Hegarty, Reginald B. *Addendum to "Starbuck" and Whaling Masters*. New Bedford: Old Dartmouth Historical Society, 1964.

_____, comp. *Returns of Whaling Vessels Sailing from American Ports, 1876–1928*. New Bedford: Old Dartmouth Historical Society, 1959.

Howell, Nathaniel R. *Long Island Whaling*. Bay Shore, New York: *Long Island Forum*, 1941.

Huster, Harrison H. "Scrimshaw: One Part Whalebone, Two Parts Nostalgia." *Antiques* 81 (1961): 122–25.

Jones, John H. *The Jones Family of Long Island*. New York: Tobias A. Wright, 1907.

Lewis, Thomas R., Jr. "From Suffield to Saybrook: An Historical Geography of the Connecticut River Valley in Connecticut before 1800." Ph.D. diss., Rutgers University, 1978. Ann Arbor: University Microfilms International, 1979.

Luce, Edward C. "Journal of a Voyage Aboard the Bark *Louisa Sears*, 1856–1858." G. W. Blunt White Library, Mystic Seaport Museum, Mystic, Connecticut.

Ludlow, E. Jones. "Journal of a Voyage Aboard the Ship *Commodore Preble*, 1842–1845." G. W. Blunt White Library, Mystic Seaport Museum, Mystic, Connecticut.

MacKay, Robert B., Geoffrey L. Rossano, and Carol A. Traynor., eds. *Between Ocean and Empire: An Illustrated History of Long Island*. Northridge, California: Windsor Publications, Inc., 1985.

Malley, Richard C. "False Teeth: New Problems with Plastic Scrimshaw." *The Log of Mystic Seaport* 32 (1980): 83–89.

_____. *Graven by the fishermen themselves: Scrimshaw in Mystic Seaport Museum*. Mystic, Connecticut: Mystic Seaport Museum, 1983.

_____. "On Shore in a Foreign Land: Mary Stark in the Kingdom of Hawaii." *The Log of Mystic Seaport* 37 (1985): 79–92.

Martin, Kenneth R. *Some Very Handsome Work: Scrimshaw at the Cape Cod National Seashore*. Eastham, Massachusetts: Eastern National Park and Monument Association, 1991.

Melville, Herman. *Moby-Dick*. New York: Harper & Brothers, 1851.

Merchant Vessels of the U.S. Washington, D.C.: Government Printing Office, 1869–.

Murphy, Robert Cushman. *The Founding of the Whaling Museum at Cold Spring Harbor, L.I., N.Y.* Cold Spring Harbor, New York: Whaling Museum Society, 1967.

_____. *Logbook for Grace: Whaling Brig Daisy, 1912–1913*. New York: Macmillan Co., 1947.

Olmstead, Frederick A. *Incidents of a Whaling Voyage*. New York: D. Appleton and Co., 1841.

"*Orion*, Logbook of the Brig, 1820–1821." G. W. Blunt White Library, Mystic Seaport Museum, Mystic, Connecticut.

Palmer, William R. "The Whaling Port of Sag Harbor." Ph.D. diss., Columbia University, 1959. Ann Arbor: University Microfilms International, 1964.

Peckham, Leslie E. *Clamtown: Cold Spring Harbor, New York*. Cold Spring Harbor, New York: author, 1962.

Penniman, Augusta. *Journal of a Whaling Voyage, 1864–1868*. Eastham, Massachusetts: Eastern National Park and Monument Association, 1988.

Penny, George G. Letters to John H. Jones, July-August 1854. Cold Spring Harbor Whaling Museum, Cold Spring Harbor, New York.

Pentley-Jones, Evan W. "Scrimshaw." *Antiques* 98 (1970): 256–62.

Prime, Nathaniel S. *History of Long Island*. New York: Robert Carter, 1845.

Rogers, Henry. "Journal of a Whaling Voyage Kept on Board the Ship

New England of New London by Henry Rogers, 1857–1859." Connecticut Historical Society, Hartford, Connecticut.

Rossano, Geoffrey L. "Prosperity on the Ways: Shipbuilding in Colonial Oyster Bay, 1745–1775." *The Long Island Historical Journal* 2 (1989): 21–28.

Rutt, Richard. *A History of Hand Knitting.* Loveland, Colorado: Interweave Press, 1987.

St. John's Church Parish Register, 1985–86. Cold Spring Harbor, New York: St. John's Church, 1986.

Salaman, R. A. *Dictionary of Tools.* New York: Charles Scribner's Sons, 1975.

Scammon, Charles M. *The Marine Mammals of the Northwestern Coast of North America.* 1874. Reprint. New York: Dover Publications, 1968.

Schmitt, Frederick P. *Mark Well the Whale!: Long Island Ships to Distant Seas.* 2nd ed. Cold Spring Harbor, New York: Whaling Museum Society, 1971.

_____. *Whale Watch: The Story of Shore Whaling off Nassau County, New York.* Cold Spring Harbor, New York: Whaling Museum Society, 1972.

Schmitt, Frederick P., Cornelis De Jong, and Frank H. Winter. *Thomas Welcome Roys.* Charlottesville: University Press of Virginia, 1980.

Sleight, Harry D. *The Whale Fishery on Long Island.* Bridgehampton, New York: Hampton Press, 1931.

Stackpole, Edouard A. *Whales & Destiny.* Amherst: University of Massachusetts Press, 1972.

Stanford, Peter. "Long Island Sound: Introduction to a Storied Waterway." *Sea History* (1989): 15–17.

Starbuck, Alexander. *History of the American Whale Fishery.* 2 vols. 1878. Reprint. New York: Argosy-Antiquarian, Ltd., 1964.

Strong, John. "Shinnecock and Montauk Whalemen." *The Long Island Historical Journal* 2 (1989): 29–41.

Taylor, Lawrence J. "Oystering on Long Island in Comparative Perspective." *The Long Island Historical Journal* 2 (1989): 64–75.

Thompson, Benjamin F. *History of Long Island.* 3 vols. 1839. 3rd ed. New York: Robert H. Dodd, 1918.

U.S. Navy Department. *Dictionary of American Naval Fighting Ships.* 7 vols. Washington, D.C.: Government Printing Office, 1959–81.

Updike, Richard W. "The walrus and the commodore – a puzzle in scrimshaw." *Antiques* 98 (1970): 263–65.

Valentine, Andrus T. "Big Manuel, Whaling Captain." *Long Island Forum* (March 1954): 49ff.

Valentine, Harriet G. *The Window on the Street.* Smithtown, New York: Exposition Press, Inc., 1981.

Valentine, Harriet G. and Andrus T. *An Island People: One Foot in the Sea, One on Shore.* Huntington, New York: authors, 1976.

Vose, Margaret L. "Selected Design Sources for Scrimshaw, a Folk Art of the New England Whaling Industry, 1775–1900." Ph.D. diss., New York University, 1992.

Watson, Arthur C. *The Long Harpoon.* New Bedford: George H. Reynolds, 1929.

Watson, Elizabeth L. "Long Island Born and Bred: The Origins and Growth of Cold Spring Harbor Laboratory." *The Long Island Historical Journal* 2 (1990): 145–62.

Webb, Robert Lloyd. "'Old Moke' Afloat: Notes on the Minstrel Origins of the Banjo at Sea." *The Log of Mystic Seaport* 35 (1984): 107–17.

_____. *On the Northwest: Commercial Whaling in the Pacific Northwest, 1790–1967.* Vancouver: University of British Columbia Press, 1988.

Weigold, Marilyn E. *The American Mediterranean: An Environmental, Economic & Social History of Long Island Sound.* Port Washington, New York: Kennikat Press, 1974.

_____. "Long Island Sound: The Great Unifier." *The Long Island Historical Journal* 2 (1990): 221–33.

Weir, Robert. "Journal of a Voyage Aboard the Bark *Clara Bell*, 1855–1858." G. W. Blunt White Library, Mystic Seaport Museum, Mystic, Connecticut.

West, Janet. "Scrimshaw in Australia with special reference to the nineteenth century. Part I." *The Great Circle* 8 (1986): 82–95.

_____. "Scrimshaw in Australia with special reference to the nineteenth century. Part II." *The Great Circle* 9 (1987): 26–39.

_____. "Scrimshaw: Recent Forgeries in Plastic." *The Mariner's Mirror* 66 (1980): 328–30.

Whaling Museum Society, Inc. *Annual Report, 1953.* Cold Spring Harbor, New York: Whaling Museum Society, Inc., 1953.

Wilson, Claggett. "Scrimshaw, the Whaleman's Art." *Antiques* 46 (1946): 278–81.

Wilson, William H. "Journal of a Voyage Aboard the Bark *Cavalier*, 1848–1850." G. W. Blunt White Library, Mystic Seaport Museum, Mystic, Connecticut.

Works Progress Administration. *Ship Registers and Enrollments of New Bedford, Mass., 1796–1939.* Boston: National Archives Project, 1940.

_____. *Whaling Masters.* New Bedford: Old Dartmouth Historical Society, 1938.

INDEX

Design by Marie-Louise Scull
Composition by Mim-G Studios, Inc., West Mystic, CT
in Veljovik Book for text and Basilica for display
Edited by Andrew W. German, West Mystic, CT
Printed by Thomson-Shore, Inc., Dexter, Michigan
on 80 lb. Ivory Mohawk Superfine text

Printed in the United States of America